SPEECH
Communication
Made Simple

A Multicultural Perspective

SECOND EDITION

Paulette Dale, Ph.D.

James C. Wolf, M.A.

Miami-Dade Community College

Longman

Speech Communication Made Simple
A Multicultural Perspective
Second Edition

Pearson Education, 10 Bank Street, White Plains, NY 10606

Editorial director: Allen Ascher
Executive editor: Louisa B. Hellegers
Director of design and production: Rhea Banker
Managing editor: Linda Moser
Development manager: Penny Laporte
Development editor: Lise Minovitz
Production editor: Mike Kemper
Text and cover design: Tracey Munz Cataldo
Production manager: Ray Keating
Manufacturing manager: Edith Pullman
Text composition: Dewey Publishing Services
Text art: V. Gene Myers and Don Martinetti
Photo credit: Page 73, Itsuo Inouye/APWide World Photos

Library of Congress-in-Publication Data

Dale, Paulette.
    Speech communication made simple: a multicultural perspective / Paulette Dale, James
C. Wolf.– 2nd ed.
        p. cm.
    Rev. ed. of: Speech communication for international students / Paulette Dale. 1988.
    ISBN 0-13-020797-7 (alk. paper)
    1. Public speaking–Problems, exercises, etc. 2. Oral communication–Problems,
exercises, etc. 3. English language–Textbooks for foreign speakers. I. Wolf, James C.,
1946- II. Dale, Paulette. Speech communication for international students. III. Title.

PN4121 .D324 2000
808.5'l–dc21

                                                                              99-059705

ISBN: 0-13-020797-7

    3 4 5 6 7 8 9 10–BB–02 01 00 99 98 97

Contents

For more than fifty collective years, the authors have been teaching speech communication classes composed of students from a wide variety of cultures. Many of their students are international students who have learned English as a second language. Most of the available texts that deal with speech communication and public speaking are written for American students and, thus, do not meet the particular speech communication needs of students with such eclectic backgrounds. Their teachers are not interested in discussing complicated communication theory and fancy terminology, such as "communication dyads," "message channels," or "transmitters." They want practical material that is relevant to the backgrounds and experiences of their students—information that their students can apply in their everyday lives.

Speech Communication Made Simple: A Multicultural Perspective is designed to meet the needs of speech communication students and their teachers around the world. It helps students to:

- develop confidence when speaking before a group
- improve their use of eye contact, posture, gestures, and voice
- orally present information, ideas, and opinions in a coherent organized fashion
- learn the basics of informative and persuasive speaking
- listen critically and objectively
- lead and participate in group discussions
- improve their understanding of interpersonal and intercultural communication

A glance at the table of contents reveals specific chapter titles and their contents.

Chapter 1: Speaking to Develop Self-Confidence is designed to help students overcome their fears and succeed at public speaking.

Chapter 2: Delivering Your Message is full of activities to help students improve their use of eye contact, posture, gestures, and voice so that they speak more effectively.

Chapter 3: Putting Your Speech Together teaches students how to organize and outline their information for their speeches.

Chapter 4: Listening includes both suggestions and exercises to improve listening skills.

Chapter 5: Speaking to Inform gives step-by-step procedures for preparing a speech that presents new information in a comprehensible and memorable way.

Chapter 6: Speaking to Persuade gives step-by-step procedures for preparing a speech that persuades others to change their beliefs, opinions, or behaviors.

Chapter 7: Participating in Group Discussions teaches students how to lead as well as how to participate in a problem-solving group discussion.

Chapter 8: Understanding Interpersonal Communication helps students avoid misunderstandings while enabling them to interact more effectively.

Chapter 9: Understanding Intercultural Communication helps students understand and appreciate the diverse beliefs and customs of people from different backgrounds in order to communicate across cultures more effectively.

Chapter 10: Thinking on Your Feet teaches students to organize their ideas quickly in order to give meaningful impromptu speeches.

Chapter 11: Using Idioms and Proverbs helps students improve their ability to both understand and use idiomatic expressions.

Chapter 12: Miscellaneous Speaking Activities contains a variety of fun and educational speech communication activities that challenge students to draw on the skills learned in previous chapters.

Teachers know that a learning-by-doing approach is the best way to learn any skill. For this reason, in addition to guiding students through the principles of speech communication, *Speech Communication Made Simple* provides a variety of exercises, activities, and assignments. Traditional exercises (such as multiple-choice exercises), innovative activities (such as communicative discussions), and extensive assignments (such as actual presentations) help students improve their communication skills in different contexts. Evaluation forms in the Appendix suggest evaluation criteria for each presentation. In addition, tips at the end of each chapter help students improve their pronunciation and intonation. The companion audiocassette provides examples of standard pronunciation and intonation, as well as listening exercises and examples of student presentations.

The supplementary *Teacher's Manual* follows the book chapter-by-chapter and provides information regarding specific assignments as well as a variety of hints about assigning, critiquing, and grading students' speech assignments. It also provides quizzes, transcripts for the listening exercises, and answer keys.

The authors' experience with thousands of students from around the world has shown that the key to lifelong feelings of confidence lies in the ability to communicate well. Developing clear and direct communication skills can lead to positive results when dealing with others, success at school and in business, and an enjoyable, rewarding life. *Speech Communication Made Simple* will enable students to become confident, effective communicators.

Acknowledgments

The authors wish to express their sincerest gratitude to the many people who assisted in developing this book:

Professor Kathleen Watson of Miami Dade Community College for writing the extremely insightful chapter on understanding intercultural communication

Professor Ellen Karsh of Florida International University for her constructive suggestions

Professor David Gravel and our other colleagues who recommended valuable improvements

The anonymous reviewers who read the material and provided valuable feedback and suggestions for improvements

Our students, for encouraging us and for giving us many practical suggestions to help us better meet their needs

Our families and friends for their support and encouragement throughout the project

Introduction

Whether you are from Miami or New York, New Delhi or Tokyo, Taiwan or Mexico City, you will find the study of speech communication to be one of the most exciting, challenging, and positive learning experiences you may ever have.

The study of speech communication, or rhetoric as it was called by the ancient Greeks, will engage you in one of the oldest academic subjects known. By studying speech communication, you are participating in an area that has been considered essential to the functioning of a democratic state and to the growth of the individual within society for over two thousand years. The study of speech communication will help you improve your knowledge, self-confidence, understanding of human nature, listening skills, critical-thinking skills, organization of thoughts, use of posture and voice, and your ability to give and accept constructive criticism.

Throughout your life, you will give many types of speeches. You will need to be able to organize your thoughts logically in order to persuade others to your way of thinking. Success in many careers, such as those in administration, government, public relations, personnel, politics, education, sales, and private industry, depends on good speech communication skills. As you can see, the study of speech communication will be applicable throughout your lifetime.

The more effort you put into the study of speech communication, the more you will benefit. Though you may be nervous about the idea of standing before an audience and making a speech, your fears will fade as you progress through this book. By the time you have finished, you will be proud of the progress you have made.

You will have many chances to speak. Some of your speaking assignments will not be graded. These assignments will give you confidence and help you to improve future speeches. Your teacher will help you learn how to select topics, make them interesting to your audience, get over problem spots, and improve your speech communication skills.

Daniel Webster, a famous American orator, once said,

> *If all my talents and powers were to be taken from me by some inscrutable Providence, and I had my choice of keeping but one, I would unhesitatingly ask to be allowed to keep the Power of Speaking, for through it, I would quickly recover all the rest.*

Let's begin!

Chapter 1

Speaking to Develop Self-Confidence

It is the beginning of the semester, and this speech class has just begun. It is natural to be nervous about speaking in front of people you've never met before. Relax—your classmates will soon become new friends and will no longer seem like strangers.

This chapter is full of helpful suggestions for presentations. Believe it or not, you are already prepared to deliver many excellent speeches. Talking about yourself, your experiences, your opinions, and your concerns or fears is the best way to do this.

You will overcome your speech fears more quickly if you have an opportunity to speak about a very familiar topic—yourself! For this reason, all the speeches in this chapter focus on you as individuals. Depending on your background and what is considered appropriate in your culture, you might be a bit reluctant to express your opinions, describe personal experiences, or share your feelings with the class. However, sharing information based on your experiences and feelings is highly appropriate in the United States and will help make your speech interesting and relevant to your listeners.

SPEECH 1: Self-Introduction

The best way for people to get to know each other in a class like this is to share autobiographical information. Your first assignment is to give a speech about yourself. Because you should be very natural and spontaneous as you speak, you will not be allowed to write your speech beforehand and read it to the class. Instead, you will choose one of the following two methods to prepare and present your speech:

- Picture Story
- Speech Preparation Worksheet

METHOD A: Picture Story

Try to think of your speech as if it were a photo album. As your eyes move from picture to picture, you recall different events in your life. Pictures make it possible for you to talk comfortably and naturally in front of a group of people. By using simple pictures as your speaking "notes," you will be able to remember what you want to say. You will be able to talk through your speech with your audience in a relaxed manner, needing only an occasional glance at your pictures to trigger your memory.

Assignment

You can use a set of basic drawings to organize your thoughts. Draw four or five different sets of pictures that will remind you what to say about yourself. Draw a different picture for each piece of information you want to share with your audience. Don't worry if you are not an artist! Simple sketches or stick drawings are fine, as long as they represent what you want to say. You may want to use color in your drawings. Whatever works for you, do it. What is important is that your pictures help you to remember to tell your audience about yourself—your background, family, interests, hobbies, and future goals. You may have heard the expression "A picture is worth a thousand words." If you use pictures, there will be no need to write a speech on paper—your pictures will be your notes!

If you have access to a computer, you might enjoy using "clip art" (cartoons or pictures from the computer) instead of drawings. Select clip art that reminds you of what you want to say about yourself. Be sure to enlarge them enough so that your audience can see them easily.

Example

Pedro would like to mention that he came to the United States two years ago and lived in New York for one year before moving to Miami. He could draw:

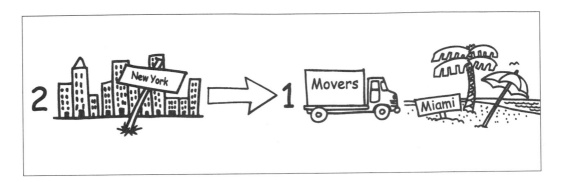

He could also select the following clip art:

Example

Stefan would like to talk about his hobbies, which include listening to music, reading books, sailing, and fishing. He could draw:

He could also select the following clip art:

Example

Noriko would like to say that she is studying photography and hopes to be a famous underwater photographer some day. She could draw:

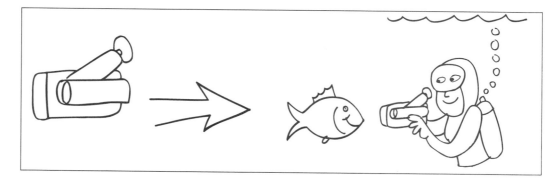

She could also select the following clip art:

METHOD B: Speech Preparation Worksheet

You can use a worksheet with questions and answers to help you organize your thoughts. When you are delivering your speech, a quick look at the worksheet will remind you of what to say about yourself.

Assignment

Answer the questions on the Self-Introduction Speech Preparation Worksheet below as completely as possible. Include as many examples as you can. Note that these questions are meant to help guide you through your speech, not limit what you say. Try to think of other information about yourself that will interest your classmates and help them learn more about you.

Self-Introduction Speech Preparation Worksheet

What is your name?[1]	
Where are you from?	
How long have you been in this country?	
Why did you come to this country?	
How many brothers or sisters do you have?[2]	
Who do you live with?	
What are you studying here?[3]	
What do you like to do in your free time?	
What hobbies or special interests do you have?	
What are your future plans and goals?	
How do you think you will benefit from taking this course?	

---

[1] Be sure to say your name clearly. If it is unusual, spell it for the class.
[2] Give names and ages.
[3] Describe the other classes you are taking.

SPEECH 2: A Personal Experience

Everybody has had experiences that are unforgettable in some way. These experiences make wonderful speech topics. When you give a speech describing a personal experience, your challenge is to make the audience relive the experience with you. If you had a happy experience, you should make your listeners feel happy. If you had a sad experience, you should make them feel sad. If you had a scary experience, they should feel afraid. If you had a funny experience, they should laugh! Make your audience feel the way you felt!

You can speak about an experience that was:

embarrassing	frightening	funny	interesting
happy	unique	uncomfortable	sad
educational	exciting	dangerous	surprising

Your goal is to speak naturally and to maintain eye contact with your listeners. As with your first speech, you cannot write it down and read it. However, you can write down your main ideas and present your speech from notes.

Two different personal experience speech assignments are described. One is for an experience you had as an adult. The other is for an experience you had as a child. Your assignment is to give a speech describing a personal experience. Whether you do Assignment A, Assignment B, or both, your task is to make the audience relive the experience with you.

Assignment A: Experience as an Adult

1. Choose an experience that you have had as an adult.

2. Using the Personal Experience Speech Preparation Worksheet on page 11, prepare notes for a speech about this experience. Be sure to include all information that will help your audience relive this experience with you.

3. Your teacher may use the form on page 188 to evaluate your speech. Look it over so you know exactly how you will be evaluated.

4. Give a two to three minute speech about your experience.

See page 7 for an example of a speech and page 8 for an example of a completed speech preparation worksheet.

Example: Francisco's Speech

INTRODUCTION

Do you think it's possible to have an experience that is dangerous, happy, sad, uncomfortable, and very scary at the same time? I had one, and I'll remember it for the rest of my life.

BODY

I escaped from Cuba three years ago at the age of eighteen with my fifteen-year-old brother José. My father wanted us to live in a free country, get a good education, and have many opportunities. In Cuba, there was no hope for a good future. My father put José and me on a raft in the middle of the night. He told us that a city called Key West in the United States was only about ninety miles north of Cuba. Our trip from Havana to Key West took three days. We were all alone without food or water. I thought we were going to starve, drown, or be eaten by sharks. I tried to comfort my brother José by telling him how much better our lives would be when we finally got to Miami. I made myself feel better by thinking that we would go to heaven and meet my parents there one day. By some miracle, the U.S. Coast Guard rescued us several miles from Key West. Relatives of ours in Miami were notified by the immigration authorities. They picked us up in Key West and we went to live with them in Miami. After two years, we saw our parents again. They finally escaped from Cuba also. That was a very happy day for me.

CONCLUSION

Now that you know my experience, I think you can understand why it was scary, sad, dangerous, uncomfortable, and finally, happy all at the same time. I didn't know it then, but it was also the most important personal experience of my life. It was important because without that experience, I wouldn't be here today in a free and wonderful country talking to all of you. Thank you.

Example: Francisco's Speech Preparation Worksheet

Personal Experience Speech Preparation Worksheet

What type of experience was it?	dangerous, scary, uncomfortable
Where were you?	beach in Cuba, middle of the night
When were you there?	3 years ago, 18 years old
Who was with you?	brother José – 15 yrs. old
What were you doing?	father put us on raft
Why were you there?	escaping to freedom
How were you feeling?	alone, scared, uncomfortable
Why did you feel that way?	no food or water, afraid of starving, sharks
What was your goal?	arrive in Key West, freedom, opportunities
How did you react?	thought of heaven and being safe there
How did the story end?	U.S. Coast Guard rescued us
Why will you never forget this experience?	I'm here today!

Assignment B: Experience as a Child

1. Choose an experience that you had as a child. The experience can be good, bad, interesting, or funny. Possible topics include:

The Time I Got Lost	The Day I Played Hooky
My Most Memorable Birthday	The Day I Ran Away from Home
My First Bicycle	An Important Lesson I Learned
A Terrible Lie I Told	My First Pet
My First Day at School	My First Childhood Sweetheart

2. Using the Speech Preparation Worksheet on page 11, prepare notes for a speech about this experience. Be sure to include all information that will help your audience relive this experience with you.

3. Your teacher may use the form on page 188 to evaluate your speech. Look it over so you know exactly how you will be evaluated.

4. Give a two to three minute speech about your experience.

 Example: Leila's Speech

INTRODUCTION

In my hands, I have a jar of honey. If you look closely, you can see part of the honey beehive in the jar. You are probably wondering why I brought a jar of honey to show you today. Every time I see honey, it reminds me of a "stinging" experience I had when I was in the sixth grade.

BODY

As a child I grew up on a farm not far from Kuala Lumpur, Malaysia. One warm summer day, my friend and I were walking home from school. We happened to see a beehive in a tree. We had just studied in school about bee colonies and how bees make honey. This was my big chance to show off to my mother and father what I had learned in school.

It looked easy! I found a stick about two meters long. I handed it to my friend and told her to sneak up to the tree and hit the hive with the stick. I said I would wait until the bees came out and then I could grab the hive and run away with it.

I soon learned a very important lesson. I learned that things don't always work out the way you plan them. My friend pushed the hive down from the tree and then ran at full speed up a nearby hill. The bees did not go after her. However, they were all over me instantly. They stung my arms; they flew down my blouse and stung me. They flew up my skirt and stung me; they got in my hair and stung me.

CONCLUSION

That was the first and last beehive that I have ever touched. Maybe now you can understand why this jar of honey I brought to show you reminds me of a very "stinging" experience!

Activity

What do you think the speaking notes that Leila used to make her speech looked like? Using her speech as a guide, complete the Personal Experience Speech Preparation Worksheet below.

Leila's Experience Speech Preparation Worksheet

What type of experience was it?	painful, unpleasant, scary
Where were you?	
When were you there?	
Who was with you?	
What were you doing?	
Why were you there?	
How were you feeling?	
Why did you feel that way?	
What was your goal?	
How did you react?	
How did the story end?	
Why will you never forget this experience?	

Use the following worksheet to prepare your notes for your personal experience speech.

Personal Experience Speech Preparation Worksheet

What type of experience was it?	
Where were you?	
When were you there?	
Who was with you?	
What were you doing?	
Why were you there?	
How were you feeling?	
Why did you feel that way?	
What was your goal?	
How did you react?	
How did the story end?	
Why will you never forget this experience?	

SPEECH 3: A Meaningful Object

Is there an object that has special meaning for you? It can be a painting, picture, piece of clothing or jewelry, or any other object. How would you describe it? Why does it have special meaning for you? The object you choose and how you describe it can give unique information about you.

Your assignment is to bring a meaningful object to class and give a speech about it.

Assignment

1. Choose an object that has special meaning for you.
2. Using the Meaningful Object Speech Preparation Worksheet on page 14, prepare notes for a speech about this object. Be sure to include all information that will help your audience understand why the object is meaningful to you.
3. Your teacher may use the form on page 189 to evaluate your speech. Look it over so you know exactly how you will be evaluated.
4. Give a two to three minute speech about the object.

 Example: Henry's Speech

INTRODUCTION

In my hand I have an object in which spirits live! They float through bluish-green stone and live forever. Would you like to see the object in which spirits live? I'll now show it to you.

BODY

This is a turquoise gemstone. It is from the southwestern United States. My father gave this to me for my sixth birthday. We were living on our hogan on the Navajo reservation. The stone is 170 years old. It's an oval shape the size of a nickel and weighs about two ounces.

This turquoise stone was first polished by my great-grandfather when he was a young man in the summer of 1831. I want you to know that turquoise is a mineral of aluminum and copper; when it is polished, it becomes a brilliant bluish green gemstone. This turquoise has a very special meaning for me because it represents the Navajo way of life. For the Navajo, all things of our earth contain the spirits of all the life forms that have touched them. When I look at this stone, its spirits help my mind to see scenes from the past: my grandfather's mud hogan, the cedar-wood fires, our struggle for survival, the desert in the summer, desert flowers and cactus, the human spirit of the Navajo. All these things belong to me in the memory of this stone.

CONCLUSION

I wanted to share this turquoise stone with all of you because we all need to realize that man must work with nature to change life for the better. I think you now understand why this magnificent object has special meaning for me. In this gemstone, many wonderful memories and spirits from the past live again.

Example: Henry's Speech Preparation Worksheet

Meaningful Object Speech Presentation Worksheet

OBJECTIVE INFORMATION	
What is it?	turquoise gemstone
How old is it?	almost 170 years old
Where is it from?	southwestern U.S.
When did you get it?	when I was 6 years old
How did you get it?	gift from my father
Why did you get it?	birthday present
What size is it?	about the size of a nickel
What shape is it?	oval
How much does it weigh?	2 ounces
What is it made of?	mineral of aluminum and copper
What features does it have?	smooth, brilliant bluish green color

SUBJECTIVE INFORMATION	
Why does it have special meaning for you?	represents Navajo way of life contains spirits of life forms
Why do you feel strongly about it?	reminds me of my ancestors' past
Why do you want to share it with the class?	We all need to realize that man must work with nature to change life for the better.

Use the following worksheet to prepare notes for your meaningful object speech.

Meaningful Object Speech Presentation Worksheet

OBJECTIVE INFORMATION

What is it?

How old is it?

Where is it from?

When did you get it?

How did you get it?

Why did you get it?

What size is it?

What shape is it?

How much does it weigh?

What is it made of?

What features does it have?

SUBJECTIVE INFORMATION

Why does it have special meaning for you?

Why do you feel strongly about it?

Why do you want to share it with the class?

SPEECH 4: A Specific Fear

Everybody is afraid of something. Anyone who says "I'm not afraid of anything" is not telling the truth. Being able to talk about something you are afraid of and to share your feelings with the class is a good way to gain confidence when speaking before an audience. Also, you might be surprised to learn that others are afraid of the same thing as you! For example, many people are afraid of:

flying in planes	being in the dark
public speaking	going to a new country
meeting new people	interviewing for a job
snakes	large dogs
taking tests	going to the hospital

Your assignment is to give a speech describing a fear.

Assignment

1. Choose a specific fear that you have.

2. Using the Specific Fear Speech Preparation Worksheet on page 16, prepare notes for a speech about this fear. Be sure to include all information that will help your audience understand your fear and the reasons for it.

3. Your teacher may use the form on page 188 to evaluate your speech. Look it over so you know exactly how you will be evaluated.

4. Give a two to three minute speech about your fear.

 Example: Humberto's Speech

INTRODUCTION

The earth was far below us. The weather was very bad. I looked at the instrument panel of the plane and saw a red warning light flashing. The pilot was very nervous. At that moment, the engine of the plane became silent!

BODY

This happened to me last year when I was flying from Cancún to Cozumel in Yucatán, Mexico. I will explain exactly what happened so you can understand why I now have a great fear of flying in small planes.

Right after we took off from the airport in Cancún, the weather turned very bad. There was a lot of thunder and lightning. It was raining very hard. It was impossible for the pilot to see out the windows of the plane. I was the only person in the plane with the pilot. After being in the air for fifteen minutes, the plane started to shake and make strange noises. All of a sudden, the engine just stopped.

When red warning lights started flashing, I became very afraid. I began to tremble and was soaked with sweat. I remember thinking that my life was about to end. I thought about how young I was and how I didn't want to die. All of a sudden, the engine started to work again. The pilot turned to me, smiled, and said, "No te preocupes!" (That means "Don't worry.")

My mother and father do not want me to fly in small planes ever again. They say I should fly on the big airlines or take a boat! I promised myself, from now on, I will do what they tell me.

CONCLUSION

I don't think I will ever fly in a small plane again. I get upset every time I think about it. I know that I will never be able to overcome this fear.

Use the following worksheet to prepare notes for your specific fear speech.

Specific Fear Speech Preparation Worksheet

What is the nature of the fear?	
When did the fear develop?	
Where did it develop?	
Why did it develop?	
How do you react when faced with this fear?	
How do your friends and family react to your fear?	
What have you done to try to overcome this fear?	

Pronunciation Tip

FINAL CONSONANTS

In English, most words end in consonant sounds. In many other languages, however, most words end in vowels. If you are not used to using final consonants in your native language, you might omit them at the ends of words in English. This can confuse your listeners, and they will have trouble understanding you.

Pronounce final consonants carefully. (Although **e** may be the last letter in a word, it is usually silent; the last sound is actually a consonant.)

Examples: made   phone   bite   have

Exercise A

The words in each of the following rows sound the same if their final consonant sounds are left off. Read each row aloud. Exaggerate your pronunciation of the final consonant in each word.

1. ca**t**   ca**p**   ca**b**   ca**n**   cal**f**
2. rac**k**   ra**t**   ra**p**   ra**g**   ra**n**
3. sou**p**   soo**n**   sui**t**   sue**d**   Sue**'s**
4. wee**k**   wee**p**   whea**t**   wee**d**   weave
5. ro**be**   ro**de**   wrote   ro**pe**   rol**l**

Exercise B

Read the following sentences aloud. Exaggerate your pronunciation of the final consonant in each boldfaced word.

1. **Have** you **had ham**?
2. I **like bright light**.
3. The **sign** is on the **side**.
4. **Doug** ate a well-**done duck**.
5. The **bag** on his **back** was **black**.

Exercise C

Choose any paragraph in this book. Circle all words that end in consonant sounds. Read the paragraph aloud. Be sure to pronounce all final consonant sounds.

Chapter 2

Delivering Your Message

William Shakespeare wrote that all speakers give two speeches at the same time: the one that is heard and the one that is seen. Believe it or not, most people are frequently more influenced by what they see than what they hear.

A professor at UCLA found that only seven percent of our credibility with listeners comes from the actual words we speak, while ninety-three percent of it comes from our vocal qualities and visual characteristics. The presidential debates between John F. Kennedy and Richard Nixon in 1960 are an excellent example of how facial expressions, gestures, eye contact, and posture can either hurt or help speakers. These debates were the first ever to be televised. The people who heard them on the radio said that Nixon won the debates. However, the people who watched them on TV insisted that Kennedy won. Kennedy's body language made a more powerful impression on the viewers than anything the candidates were actually saying.

What is *body language*? Body language means "posture, eye contact, facial expressions, and gestures." Your body language, as well as your speech patterns, reflect how you feel about yourself. It also affects how others react to you. It can help you convey an aura of confidence, or it can make you appear uncertain before you even open your mouth.

People will pay attention to you and your words if you look them in the eye, improve your posture and use of gestures, and use decisive-sounding speech patterns. This chapter will introduce you to techniques for delivering your message in both formal and informal speaking.

Posture Talks

Your posture tells how you feel about yourself. It can say, "I'm timid and afraid of my own shadow. Don't listen to me; just ignore me." On the other hand, your posture can send the message, "Listen to me. I know what I'm talking about." Looking down and refusing to face people directly gives the impression that you're ashamed or embarrassed. Cocking your head to the side, rounding your shoulders, dropping your chin, clutching your arms across your shoulders, wrapping your arms around your body, or clasping your hands tightly in front of you can also make you appear insecure or defeated.

Observe the body language of the following individuals. Who looks the most confident?

If you said Cheryl, you're right. What is it about Cheryl's posture that causes her to project courage and confidence?

Diane   Carl   Cheryl   Simon

When giving a speech, here are five ways you can radiate confidence and strength of character even before you open your mouth:

- Keep your spine straight and rotate your shoulders back.
- Keep your head erect.
- Keep your hands at your sides with your fingers open or slightly curled.
- Keep both feet flat on the floor and slightly apart.
- If you are using a lectern, be careful not to bend over it or lean on it. Instead, stand naturally erect and gently rest your hands on the sides of the lectern.

Here are three ways you can project confidence when sitting and listening:

- Sit straight while leaning forward slightly to show interest in the speaker.
- Rest your hands lightly in your lap or on the arms of your chair.
- Keep your legs together with your feet flat on the floor or crossed at the ankles.

Improving your posture isn't difficult. It's as simple as doing what your mother probably used to tell you all the time: "Stand up straight," "Stop slouching," or "Sit up in your chair!" The old trick of walking around your house with a book on your head still works wonders.

Remember, your speech starts before you even say one word! Your audience takes notice of you before you begin to speak. They watch you as you walk to the front of the room. They form an impression about your level of confidence, your ability, and your credibility during your short trip to the podium.

Manolo Martín-Vásquez, a famous Spanish matador, said, "The most important lesson in courage is physical, not mental. From the age of twelve, I was taught to walk in a way that produces courage. The mental part comes later." If you want to appear confident when you walk up to the podium, walk the walk of the matador!

Activity

In class, practice the walk of the matador.

1. Walk to the front of the classroom with your head up, your spine straight, and your shoulders back.

2. Spend a few moments standing at the lectern looking directly at your audience.

3. Say "good morning" or "good afternoon."

4. Walk back to your seat with your head up, your spine straight, and your shoulders back.

Look Them in the Eye

Eye contact customs vary from culture to culture. In some eastern cultures, women are expected to lower their eyes in communication situations. In other cultures it is a sign of respect to lower one's eyes when speaking to older people.

In Japan, audiences look down in order to show respect for a speaker. The speaker may acknowledge the audience's humility by looking down as well. Japanese school children are taught to look at their teacher's neck. As adults, they show respect by lowering their eyes when speaking to a superior. On the other hand, American children are taught just the opposite. Their parents and teachers often tell them, "Look at me when I'm speaking."

In some Latin American and African cultures, prolonged eye contact from a person of lower status is considered disrespectful. In Brazil, for example, the less powerful person generally glances away from the more important individual.

In the United States making eye contact with your listeners is absolutely essential for becoming an effective communicator. Good eye contact is taken to mean that you are open and honest, while looking away is interpreted as an indication of insincerity or dishonesty. Looking your listeners directly in the eye can be more effective than the words you say. It encourages them to pay attention to you, to respond to you, and to respect you. When you avoid eye contact, people may get the impression that you are anxious, dishonest, embarrassed, or ashamed. The right amount of eye contact indicates that you have confidence in yourself and what you are saying. If you look at the floor or out the window, your listeners will think that you are not interested in your topic or in them! Good eye contact also allows you to "read" your listeners' faces to get feedback on how they like your speech. Moreover, when you look directly at your listeners, their nods, gestures, and smiles let you know that they understand and are interested in what you're saying.

If the thought of maintaining eye contact with one or more people seems disconcerting, remember that effective eye contact does not mean staring at a person. It means shifting your focus to and from a person's eyes.

Activity A

With a conversation partner, take turns talking about any topic for two to three minutes. For example, you can talk about your weekend, your summer vacation, or a new pet.

1. Focus on your partner's left eye for four seconds.
2. Shift your focus to your partner's right eye for four seconds.
3. Look at your partner's entire face for four seconds.
4. Glance at your partner's nose for four seconds, chin for four seconds, and forehead for four seconds.
5. Repeat steps 1–4.

Activity B

Practice walking confidently to the front of the room and looking at your audience as you speak about any topic.

1. Walk the walk of the matador to the front of the room.

2. Greet your audience.

3. Speak about your topic for two to three minutes. As you speak, move your eyes from one section of the audience to another. Look at one person for four to five seconds, then another person for four to five seconds.

4. Thank your audience.

Activity C

In small groups, discuss the questions below. When you have finished, share your ideas with the class.

1. As a child, what were you taught about eye contact?

2. How did you feel when participating in Activity A as the speaker? as the listener?

3. How did you feel when participating in Activity B as the speaker? as the listener?

4. What were your listeners' reactions to your conscious efforts to maintain eye contact with them?

Facial Expressions and Gestures

Facial expressions and gestures also vary greatly in different cultures. In some societies, speakers limit facial expressions and inhibit gestures. In others, gestures are used frequently.

For example, in Japan, speakers rarely vary facial expressions or gestures. Brazilian and French speakers use gestures with greater frequency than North Americans, and Italian speakers tend to gesture more than other cultural groups.

During a business presentation in Japan, a speaker who smiles or chuckles might convey confusion or embarrassment to his or her listeners. On the other hand, an American speaker might purposely laugh to express irony or humor.

Speakers in the United States use a variety of gestures and facial expressions to help maintain the listeners' interest in their message and to appear relaxed and in control.

Facial Expressions

If you smile before you speak, you give your listeners the impression that you are confident and looking forward to speaking. Don't fake a big "politician-type" smile! A small, natural smile will be fine. A smile is a good way to establish rapport with your audience and to help put both you and your audience at ease. Other facial expressions can be used to convey different emotions. Try to change your facial expressions during your speech to convey the emotions that you feel.

Movement

Listeners find it extremely distracting to watch speakers nervously twirl strands of hair with their fingers, fiddle with earrings, necklaces, or other items of jewelry, or constantly push slipping eyeglasses up on their noses. If you have long hair, tie it back during your presentation so you won't be tempted to play with it or to fling it away from your face. While speaking, don't hide your hands in your pockets and jingle your keys or loose change. Keep your hands at your sides. On the other hand, don't stand "frozen" in one place for your entire speech. If you're nervous, take a few steps to your right or left while speaking. This will help you to relax and move naturally.

Gestures

Important points in your speech can be emphasized by using gestures—hand and arm movements. Here are some examples:

Size: Show the width or height of an object by using your hands.

Enthusiasm for an idea: Punch the air with your fist to show your enthusiasm for a new policy.

Symbolic action: Wave your hand in greeting to show how you felt when you saw a long-lost friend.

Location: Point your index finger to show a specific location on a map or use your hand in a sweeping motion to show a wider area.

Activity

Experiment with the following body language and facial expressions at home while looking at yourself in a full-length mirror. This practice will help you become aware of how you appear to others when you talk to them.

BODY LANGUAGE

1. Cover your mouth with your hand while speaking.
2. Sway back and forth on your feet.
3. Cross your arms in front of you.
4. Wrap your arms around your body.
5. Tilt your head.
6. Twirl a strand of hair around your finger.
7. Play with a button or an item of jewelry.
8. Shake your head excessively while speaking.
9. Cross your legs.
10. Look down at your feet.

FACIAL EXPRESSIONS

1. Look happy.
2. Look worried.
3. Wrinkle your eyebrows.
4. Look interested.
5. Squint your eyes.
6. Bite your lip.
7. Lick your lips.
8. Look angry.
9. Look unhappy.
10. Look neutral.

Using Visual Aids

American audiences enjoy eye-catching, colorful visual aids. They relate well to product samples, charts, graphs, photographs, and working models of objects and equipment.

Any visual aids you use should portray Americans as being a diverse group. As long as you depict people of any age, gender, race, or religion favorably, almost anything goes. The sections entitled "Preparing Visual Aids" in Chapters 4 and 5 will help you to prepare and use visual aids that will make your information more interesting and easier to understand and remember.

Are You Asking Me or Telling Me?

This is a declarative sentence? The way some people speak, it may as well be!

Your voice has a natural upward inflection when you ask a question, such as, "Would you like coffee?" If you use the upward inflection too much, you'll sound unsure of yourself and your listeners won't take you seriously. You'll sound like you're asking a question rather than making a statement. This is exactly what happened to Sally.

Sally was twenty-eight years old and a new math teacher at a large junior high school. She had discipline problems with her students and was not as effective a teacher as she knew she could be. At lunch one day, she discussed her problem with Judd, the speech teacher. After observing her teach a lesson, Judd diagnosed the problem. Her classes frequently ignored her instructions because she always sounded like she was asking rather than telling her students to do assignments. "Do the exercises on page thirty-five for homework?" "Study your formulas for the quiz Tuesday?"

Judd helped Sally get rid of her "up talk." Once she learned to drop the pitch of her voice at the end of sentences, her students began to take her seriously. They realized that she meant what she said.

People won't listen to you if your voice turns every sentence into a question. Why should they? Using an upward inflection at the end of your statements tells your listeners that you don't know what you're talking about. After all, how much faith would you have in a doctor who says, "Your wrist isn't sprained? It's broken? I need to operate?"

In written form, punctuation marks tell us whether a sentence is a question or a statement.

> **Example:** It's raining?
> It's raining.

In speaking, upward intonation generally signals a question and downward intonation generally signals a statement.

 ## Activity

Practice saying the following pairs of sentences aloud. Use downward intonation for the sentences that end with exclamation marks. Use upward intonation for those that end with question marks. Notice how downward intonation makes you sound certain, while upward intonation makes you sound doubtful.

1. a) We need a better cafeteria!
   b) We need a better cafeteria?

2. a) I'm going to get an "A" in this class!
   b) I'm going to get an "A" in this class?

3. a) I deserve a raise!
   b) I deserve a raise?

4. a) I'm a good student!
   b) I'm a good student?

5. a) I worked hard on the project!
   b) I worked hard on the project?

6. a) Susana is my best friend!
   b) Susana is my best friend?

7. a) Rafael doesn't like pizza!
   b) Rafael doesn't like pizza?

8. a) We saw Avi's new car!
   b) We saw Avi's new car?

Discard Those Disclaimers and Apologies

Too many speakers use disclaimers or apologies for their comments before they even begin their speeches. Disclaimers are remarks that weaken or diminish the impact of what the speaker is about to say. Likewise, when the speaker apologizes for a speech beforehand, he or she makes an admission that it is less than perfect before the members of the audience have the chance to judge the speech for themselves. They can kill good ideas before they're even born.

In some cultures, beginning a presentation with an apology is a sign of humility. Japanese speakers, for example, frequently begin with an apology before expressing their ideas. They tend to belittle themselves, their products, their companies, and their accomplishments as being humble and barely significant.

In the United States, speakers who use disclaimers and apologies when they speak sound unsure of themselves. Don't begin your speech by saying, "I'm sorry I didn't have more time to prepare," or "I'm not an expert on this topic." Comments like these reduce your credibility and diminish the value of your opinions and feelings. Avoid these types of remarks. Deliver your message without either first apologizing or first disclaiming your words.

Silence Is Golden

Expressions and noises such as "You know?" "You know what I mean?" "Um!" "Er!" "Uh!" are called "vocal fillers." They distract from the speaker's message and signal that he or she is uneasy. They cause the speaker to appear even more nervous than he or she really is.

Assertive, confident speakers know the importance of deliberate silences when they speak. Speakers who use well-placed pauses and avoid vocal fillers are regarded as being more confident and knowledgeable than speakers who don't. For some reason, many people are uneasy with silence and feel that every second needs to be filled with sound. However, silence can be golden. You can use a moment of silence to think about what you want to say next or to recollect your ideas if you temporarily forget what you want to say. Silences or pauses between your comments also give your listeners time to consider what you've just said.

In *Speak With Power and Grace*, speech expert Linda D. Swink writes, "I firmly believe the first two words in the English language are, 'Well, ah!' Watch any TV news program or game show when the reporter or host asks a question. You'll notice the person responding will begin by saying, 'Well, ah.' And the ahs don't stop there; they are peppered throughout our speech unknowingly. Filler words are distracting, annoying, and unprofessional."

Don't fill every pause with unnecessary vocal fillers. Learn to feel comfortable with silences between your thoughts and ideas.

Activity A

Practice tape-recording and listening to your conversations at home.

1. Tape-record yourself while having conversations in as many situations as possible.

2. Listen to the recording.

3. Analyze how you sound. Become aware of any distracting vocal habits (e.g., up talk, disclaimers, or vocal fillers).

4. Be prepared to discuss your observations in class.

Activity B

Practice giving an impromptu (unprepared) speech in front of the class.

1. Go to the front of the class.

2. You will be assigned a simple topic, such as one of the following:

apples	pens	chairs	rocks	trees
dogs	bicycles	rain	eyes	teeth

3. Without preparing, speak about the topic for sixty seconds. Concentrate on speaking fluently and avoiding pauses, hesitations, and other vocal fillers. Don't worry about organization.

Activity C

At home, practice tape-recording and listening to yourself giving a short speech.

1. Choose a topic from Activity B on page 27 or your own topic.

2. Tape-record yourself while speaking fluently about the topic for at least sixty seconds.

3. Listen to the recording.

4. Analyze how you sound. Become aware of any distracting vocal habits (e.g., up talk, disclaimers, or vocal fillers).

Write for the Ear

The speech delivery style of Europeans and Asians tends to be very formal. Speakers of these cultures often read oral presentations from carefully written manuscripts.

On the other hand, American speakers are generally more informal relative to speakers in other cultures. American audiences prefer a natural, spontaneous delivery that conveys a lively sense of communication. They don't relate well to speakers who read from a manuscript. If you use an outline of your ideas instead of a prepared text, your speech will not only sound more natural, but you will also be able to establish better rapport with your listeners and keep their attention. For specific information about how to organize and outline your speech, see Chapter 3: Putting Your Speech Together. In addition, example speech outlines are presented throughout this book.

The language and style you use when making an oral presentation should not be the same as the language and style you use when writing. Well-written information that is meant to be read does not work as well when it is heard. It is therefore important for you to adapt written texts or outlines for presentations. For example, I once heard a speaker say, "Several examples of what is described above are listed below." I wanted to scream, "Above what? Above your head? Listed where? Below what? Below your feet? I'm not reading your information! I'm listening to it!" It would have been much more effective for the speaker to say, "I will now give you several examples of what I just described."

Good speakers are much more informal when speaking than when writing. They also use their own words and develop their own speaking styles. Whenever possible, they use short words. Listeners appreciate it when speakers use simple, everyday words in a presentation. One advantage is that it is much easier for speakers to pronounce short words correctly. Another is that long and sophisticated vocabulary choices make listening more difficult. For example, which would you rather hear?

The facilitation of a listener's comprehension of information can be better accomplished by the speaker's utilization of succinct words.

or

Listeners understand information more easily when a speaker uses short words.

Good speakers use short sentences. If you can say a sentence in one breath, it's probably a good length. Try to keep your spoken sentences under fifteen words, and never use fifteen words when ten will do. Unnecessary words detract from your message. Long sentences are difficult for listeners to follow and hard for speakers to say.

Activity

The following sentences are loaded with unnecessary words. Rewrite them using as few words as possible.

Example

The rights for distribution of the book in thirty countries had been sold by him as well as the rights for distribution in twelve different languages.

He sold rights to distribute the book in thirty countries and twelve
different languages.

1. It is unfortunate that the number of students enrolled at the college this year has been reduced.

2. It was our travel agent who recommended that we go through the process of changing our plans and visit Spain in addition to the rest of our travel itinerary.

3. There is a tendency for teenagers and their mothers and fathers to be in conflict about their curfews.

4. It is my understanding that students and faculty members are not in agreement about the scheduling of final exams.

5. At this point in time, my initial trip to Europe is fondly remembered by me.

Now that you know the basic principles of effective delivery, the next step is to practice your speech. The following tips will help you rehearse effectively:

- Begin practicing several days before your presentation.
- Choose a location to practice that is private, quiet, and free from distractions (e.g., an empty classroom or your bedroom).
- Allow yourself enough time to rehearse your speech from start to finish.
- Practice your speech in front of a full-length mirror. Monitor your eye contact and body language.
- Tape record or videotape yourself while practicing. When you listen to the recording, check for errors in content and delivery. Write down any corrections and work on improving your speech the next time you practice.
- Practice your speech in front of a few friends or family members. Pretend that you are actually delivering your speech in front of your classmates. Ask your "audience" to comment on various aspects of your delivery.

Pronunciation Tip

ENDING: -ed

In written English, the ending **-ed** forms the past tense of regular verbs. However, in spoken English, the **-ed** ending can have three different pronunciations. It can sound like [t] (as in *stopped*); it can sound like [d] (as in *lived*); or it can sound like [ɪd] (as in *loaded*).

 Exercise A

The ending **-ed** always sounds like [t] when the last sound in the present tense verb is voiceless. The sounds [p], [k], [f], [s], [ʃ] (as in *wash*), and [tʃ] (as in *watch*) are voiceless.

Examples: talk**ed** cross**ed** laugh**ed**

Read the following words and sentences aloud. Be sure to pronounce the **-ed** in the past tense verb like [t].

1. look**ed**
2. miss**ed**
3. stopp**ed**
4. work**ed**
5. pick**ed**
6. wish**ed**
7. Mom bak**ed** a pie.
8. He finish**ed** early.
9. Tara stopp**ed** singing.

Exercise B

The ending **-ed** always sounds like [d] when the last sound in the present tense verb is voiced. All vowels and the consonant sounds [b], [g], [v], [m], [n], [l], [r], and [ð] (as in *breathe*) are voiced.

Examples: liv**ed**   turn**ed**   play**ed**

Read the following words and sentences aloud. Be sure to pronounce the **-ed** in the past tense verb like [d].

1. lov**ed**
2. stay**ed**
3. fill**ed**
4. burn**ed**
5. fibb**ed**
6. cri**ed**
7. We play**ed** a game.
8. He mov**ed** again.
9. I mail**ed** a letter.

 Exercise C

The ending **-ed** always sounds like [ɪd] when the last sound in the present tense verb is [t] or [d].

Examples: want**ed**   rest**ed**   end**ed**

Read the following words and sentences aloud. Be sure to pronounce the **-ed** in the past verb like [ɪd].

1. end**ed**
2. add**ed**
3. hunt**ed**
4. want**ed**
5. need**ed**
6. paint**ed**
7. I rest**ed** at home.
8. The car start**ed**.
9. He avoid**ed** his boss.

Chapter 3

Putting Your Speech Together

"Where do I begin?" is a question students often ask when faced with the task of writing a speech. This chapter will help you organize and outline your thoughts and your information so that you can deliver your speech logically and clearly.

Every speech needs a topic and a purpose. Before you can begin gathering and organizing information for your speech, select a topic and clearly define your purpose. For example, your purpose might be to inform people about an unfamiliar topic or to persuade them to change their opinion about an issue. Chapters 4 and 5 will help you to choose a topic and define your specific purpose.

Preparing the Speech

Every speech has three parts: the introduction, the body, and the conclusion. Which part of a speech do you think you prepare first? Write the numbers 1, 2, and 3 to indicate which part of your speech you should prepare first, second, and third.

____ Introduction

____ Body

____ Conclusion

The correct answers may surprise you. They are b, c, and a. First, you should write the body of your speech. Then, you should write the conclusion. Finally, you should write the introduction.

Step 1: Prepare the Body

The body of a speech contains three or four sections related to the topic. It includes an outline of the major ideas, and it also has information that supports and clarifies those ideas.

To prepare the body, first list subtopics that you might include in your speech. Write them as you think of them. Some ideas will be important, and some will not. At this time, just concentrate on writing all the ideas you can think of that relate to the topic and purpose of your speech.

Example: Speech Entitled "Having a Happy Marriage"
- Choose the best honeymoon vacation.
- Discuss important financial matters together.
- Be courteous to each other.
- Learn to compromise.
- Bring up your children well.
- Respect your spouse's property.
- Buy a nice home together.

Example: Speech Entitled "Applying for a Job"
- Choose an appropriate wardrobe.
- Behave appropriately during the personal interview.
- Write a résumé.
- Find the desired position.
- Schedule appointments.
- Get a flexible work schedule.
- Learn new skills.

Second, narrow your list of subtopics. Review your list and select the three or four subtopics that will best develop your speech in the time allowed. These subtopics will become the main headings of your speech.

Example: Speech Entitled "Having a Happy Marriage"
- ~~Choose the best honeymoon vacation.~~
- Discuss important financial matters together.
- Be courteous to each other.
- Learn to compromise.
- ~~Bring up your children well.~~
- Respect your spouse's property.
- ~~Buy a nice home together.~~

Example: Speech Entitled "Applying for a Job"
- ~~Choose an appropriate wardrobe.~~
- Behave appropriately during the personal interview.
- Write a résumé.
- Find the desired position.
- Schedule appointments.
- ~~Get a flexible work schedule.~~
- ~~Learn new skills.~~

Third, order your subtopics logically so that one leads naturally into the next one.

Example: Speech Entitled "Having a Happy Marriage"
- I. Respect your spouse's property.
- II. Be courteous to each other.
- III. Discuss important financial matters together.
- IV. Learn to compromise.

Example: Speech Entitled "Applying for a Job"
- I. Find the desired position.
- II. Write a résumé.
- III. Schedule appointments.
- IV. Behave appropriately during the personal interview.

Detailed explanations about different ways to organize your speech are in Chapter 5: Speaking to Inform.

Fourth, develop your subtopics with factual information, logical proof, and visual aids. If your subtopics are supported and well-organized, your sections will be interesting and your listeners will better understand and remember your speech.

The sections entitled "Gathering Information" in Chapters 5 and 6 give specific information about how to develop your subtopics by using your own knowledge, your own experience, concrete examples, quotes from experts, visual aids, and information from books, newspapers, magazines, and the Internet. The section entitled "Outlining Your Speech" on pages 38–42 of this chapter shows how to organize and outline this information.

Step 2: Prepare the Conclusion

The conclusion includes:

- a summary of the main points
- final remarks to end the speech gracefully

A good summary reminds your audience what you said. To summarize your speech, briefly review your purpose and repeat the main ideas. After your summary, conclude with a memorable statement that will leave your audience thinking about what you've said.

Example: Speech Entitled "Having a Happy Marriage"

   I. Now you know four factors that are important in order to have a happy marriage.

      A. Respect your spouse's property.

      B. Be courteous to each other.

      C. Discuss important financial matters together.

      D. Learn to compromise.

   II. So, be sure to follow these four guidelines for a long and happy marriage. Please don't forget to invite me to your fiftieth wedding anniversary!

The sections entitled "Prepare a Summary" and "Prepare Memorable Concluding Remarks" in Chapter 5 provide many examples of ways to effectively conclude speeches.

Step 3: Prepare the Introduction

Your introduction should have:

- an attention-getting opener (or "hook")
- a preview of the body

A good introduction captures the listeners' attention immediately and makes them interested in the rest of the speech. It also alerts them to what they can expect to hear in the presentation and helps them to follow the information easily. Powerful ways to begin your speech include telling a brief story, asking a question to arouse curiosity, or shocking your audience with a startling quote or fact. After you have delivered your introduction, tell your listeners the main points of your speech by briefly previewing its main sections.

Example: Speech Entitled "Applying for a Job"

I. What I'm about to tell you could change your life! If you listen carefully to what I have to say, you'll be able to land the job of your dreams.

II. I'm going to discuss four important aspects to consider when applying for a job.

    A. Find the desired position.

    B. Write a successful résumé.

    C. Schedule appointments.

    D. Behave appropriately during the personal interview.

Example: Speech Entitled "Electronic Espionage in Business and Industry"

I. In my hand I have the prototype of a new computer-enhanced electronic microphone that is so sensitive it can pick up the sound of a fly walking across a pane of glass a block away. Sounds incredible, right? But it's true!

II. My presentation will cover three aspects of electronic espionage in business and industry.

    A. Different types of devices used in electronic espionage

    B. Ethical implications of using electronic espionage

    C. Advantages of using such technology in business and industry

The sections entitled "Prepare a Preview" and "Prepare an Attention-Getting Opener" in Chapter 5 provide additional information about preparing introductions.

Outlines

An outline makes it easy for you to deliver your speech. It assures you that you have organized your ideas and helps you remember all your information. With a good outline, you'll never have to worry about forgetting what you want to say. Even when you're not giving a speech, an outline can make your life easier. For example, if you have several errands to do after class, you could organize them as follows:

Example

   I. Post office

  II. Grocery store

 III. Gas station

 IV. Bank

When one item doesn't depend on another, any random order of organization is fine. However, suppose your car's gas gauge reads "empty" and you don't have any money to pay for gas. You would have to change your organizational pattern. Your new outline would look like this:

Example

   I. Bank

  II. Gas Station

 III. Post Office

 IV. Grocery Store

You may have a lot on your mind. As a result, you may forget what you want to do at each of the places you need to go to. No problem! Add specific details to each point of your outline:

Example

  I. Bank

    A. Cash check from Uncle Mario.

    B. Deposit paycheck into savings account.

    C. Pay fine for bouncing a check.

 II. Gas station

    A. Fill up tank.

    B. Check water in battery.

    C. Check oil level.

    D. Put air in tires.

As you can see, the key to outlining is to identify subtopics and add specific details. With such an outline, you will never arrive home having forgotten something you had to do. Do this for your speeches and you will never again have the worry "What if I forget what I was going to say?"

Outlining Your Speech

Now that you have gathered enough information to prepare the introduction, body, and conclusion of your speech, you are ready to reorganize it and outline it. A good outline meets four basic requirements:

- Each supporting point relates to the main point.
- Each supporting point contains only one idea.
- Supporting points are not repeated or restated.
- Each supporting parallel point has an equal level of importance.

Each supporting point relates to the main point.

Which supporting idea in the example below does not belong? Why not?

    I. Alcoholism is an international problem.
        A. Russia has a high alcoholism rate.
        B. France has the highest alcoholism rate in Europe.
        C. Alcoholics have more car accidents than nondrinkers.
        D. Japan has a severe juvenile alcoholism problem.

The answer is C. Although it is an interesting fact, it is not directly related to the main point—alcoholism is an international problem.

Each supporting point contains only one idea.

What is wrong with the example below?

    I. Small cars are better than large cars.
        A. They are less expensive and easier to park.
        B. They get better gas mileage.

Point A contains two separate ideas. The information should be outlined as follows:

    I. Small cars are better than large cars.
        A. They are less expensive.
        B. They are easier to park.
        C. They get better gas mileage.

Supporting points are not repeated or restated.

What is wrong with the example below?

    I. Students dislike the school cafeteria.
       A. There is very little to choose from.
       B. The food is too expensive.
       C. The menu is extremely limited.

Points A and C repeat the same idea. The example below contains three supporting points that express different ideas.

    I. Students dislike the school cafeteria.
       A. There is very little to choose from.
       B. The food is too expensive.
       C. The eating utensils are always dirty.

Each supporting parallel point has an equal level of importance.

What is wrong with the example below?

    I. Sales in South America have fallen drastically.
       A. Colombia
       B. Lima
       C. Ecuador

Points A and C are countries. Point B is a city. The points should be all cities or all countries. The information should be outlined as follows:

    I. Sales in South America have fallen drastically.
       A. Colombia
       B. Peru
       C. Ecuador

Exercise

Write the letter of the choice that best describes what is wrong with each of the outlines that follow.

    a. Incorrect. Each supporting point does not relate to the main point.
    b. Incorrect. Each supporting point does not contain only one idea.
    c. Incorrect. Supporting points are repeated or restated.
    d. Incorrect. Each supporting parallel point does not have an equal level of importance.
    e. Correct.

Example A

_b_ I. Polyester is better than cotton.
   A. It is less expensive and easier to wash.
   B. It lasts longer.
   C. It requires less ironing.

Example B

_a_ I. Madrid has many fascinating places.
   A. The Prado Museum houses priceless works of art.
   B. The Plaza del Sol is exciting.
   C. Madrid has the best sangria in Spain.

1. ____ I. Tourists buy many products in the United States.
   A. They buy camera equipment.
   B. They buy toasters.
   C. They purchase kitchen appliances.
   D. They purchase designer clothing.

2. ____ I. There are many advantages to freeze-drying.
   A. Foods keep their nutritional value almost indefinitely.
   B. Freeze-dried foods don't require refrigeration.
   C. It's a relatively new technology.
   D. Freeze-dried foods maintain their flavor longer than regular frozen foods.

3. ____ I. There are many good ways to invest your money.
   A. Stocks
   B. Mutual funds
   C. Real estate
   D. Corporate bonds

4. ____ I. The bank offers a variety of accounts.
   A. Certificates of deposit
   B. Checking and money-market savings accounts
   C. Retirement accounts

5. ____ I. Attending college is very expensive.
   A. Tuition fees are quite high.
   B. It costs a fortune to go to college today.
   C. Textbooks are extremely expensive.

6. ____ I. Juvenile delinquency is a nationwide problem.
        A. The Northeast
        B. New York
        C. The Southwest
        D. The Midwest

7. ____ I. Cats make wonderful pets.
        A. They are easy to care for.
        B. They were worshipped in ancient Egypt.
        C. Cats provide excellent companionship.

8. ____ I. Reasons for students' parking problems on campus
        A. There are too many students with cars.
        B. Many outsiders illegally park in the lots.
        C. Students could take the bus to campus.

9. ____ I. Gambling takes many forms.
        A. Casino gambling
        B. Horse racing
        C. Lotteries

10. ____ I. Ways to fight inflation
        A. Buy things on sale.
        B. Comparison shop for the best prices.
        C. The annual inflation rate is approximately five percent.

Activity

What is wrong with the outlines below? Rewrite each one so that it meets the four basic requirements of a good outline:

- Each supporting point relates to the main point.
- Each supporting point contains only one idea.
- Supporting points are not repeated or restated.
- Each supporting parallel point has an equal level of importance.

1. Since it lasts longer and costs less, polyester is better than silk; in addition, it is easier to care for.

    I. It may be washed twice as many times before wearing out, and its color doesn't fade as quickly.
    II. It doesn't have to be dry-cleaned, and ironing is unnecessary.

2. The United States exports products to countries on several continents. These include South America, Brazil, Argentina, and Asia.

   I. Other places receiving U.S. exports are Japan, China, and Colombia.

   II. Europe, Spain, France, and Germany receive U.S. exports.

3. There are many things to do on a visit to Mexico City, including going shopping and visiting interesting places.

   I. You will enjoy visits to Chapultepec Park, the Aztec pyramids in Teotihaucán, the world-renowned Museum of Anthropology, and the Palace of Fine Arts, where you can see art exhibitions and the Ballet Gran Folklórico de México.

   II. You can shop for native crafts such as colorful embroidered blouses, handwoven rugs, and handmade pottery.

   III. You can also shop for items of onyx such as ashtrays, vases, and bookends. Silver lovers can buy beautiful sterling silver pieces such as serving trays, picture frames, and key chains.

Transitions

Transitions make it easy for your listeners to follow your plan for your speech. They remind your audience where you've been and tell them where you're going.

Think of transitions in a speech as "signposts" along a highway as you travel from one city to another. For example, let's say that you and a friend are en route from Miami to Disney World in Orlando. After driving for an hour you see a sign that says, "Welcome to Ft. Lauderdale." Shortly after that you see another sign that says "Orlando, 200 Miles." You know where you've been and how far you are from your destination. The signposts reassure you that you are on the right road, and they help you to stay on track.

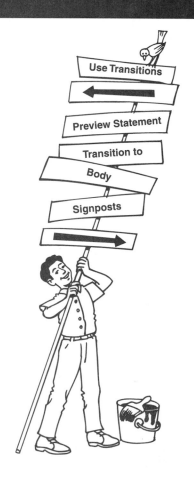

Just as signposts on a highway are important, so are transitions in a speech. Transitions tell your audience that something new or important is about to happen in your speech.

Transition after the Introduction

Every speech needs a transition after the introduction. This transition should signal that the main part of the speech is about to begin. For example, look at the outline for "A Fabulous Fantasia Cruise" on pages 44–47. After the introduction, the following transition signals the first section of the body:

First, you'll be pleased to learn about the comfortable cabins that will be your rooms for the week.

Transitions within the Body

Transitions are also needed between each section of the body. This kind of transition generally consists of two separate sentences that provide two important functions:

- to review the information just presented
- to preview the next section

For example, look at the outline for "A Fabulous Fantasia Cruise" on pages 44–47. After talking about guest accommodations, the following transition is used before talking about the ship's facilities:

Now you can see how comfortable you'll be while in your cabin. However, the ship has many facilities for you to enjoy when you leave your cabin.

After talking about the ship's facilities, this next transition is used before discussing ports of call:

As you can see, the ship has many facilities for you to enjoy while onboard. You will need to get off the ship in order to visit the four exciting ports of call.

After discussing ports of call, the following transition is used before introducing shore visit activities:

You now know which exotic places you'll be visiting. You will have a choice of many fun things to do while on shore.

Finally, after talking about shore visit activities, the transition below is used before discussing shipboard activities:

We hope the shore visit activities won't tire you out too much. You'll need your energy, because once you're back on the ship many other activities await you!

Transition before the Conclusion

Every speech needs a transition before the conclusion. This last transition acts as a signal that the speech is about to end. For example, look at the outline for "A Fabulous Fantasia Cruise" on pages 44–47. The last section is about shipboard activities. The following transition links the body and the conclusion:

With all these great onboard activities, you might not even want to leave the ship at all!

Activity

The partial outline below includes the introduction and conclusion of a speech entitled "A Fabulous Fantasia Cruise." Some of the headings and supporting ideas have already been filled in. Use the list of **Missing Headings and Supporting Ideas** on page 47 to complete the outline.

INTRODUCTION

I. Are you wondering what to do for your next vacation? I have the perfect solution for all of you. Why not take a cruise?

II. I'm going to tell you about five highlights you can expect on a fabulous Fantasia Cruise.

    A. Luxurious guest accommodations

    B. Excellent shipboard facilities

    C. Exotic ports of call

    D. Interesting shore visit activities

    E. Fun shipboard activities

TRANSITION: *First, you'll be pleased to learn about the comfortable cabins that will be your rooms for the week.*

BODY

I. _____

    A. Fully air-conditioned cabins

    B. _____

    C. _____

    D. _____

TRANSITION: *Now you can see how comfortable you'll be while in your cabin. However, the ship has many facilities for you to enjoy when you leave your cabin.*

II. Ship's Facilities

    A. _____

    B. Swinging disco open all night

    C. _____

    D. _____

TRANSITION: *As you can see, the ship has many facilities for you to enjoy while onboard. You will need to get off the ship in order to visit the four exciting ports of call.*

III. _____

    A. _____

    B. _____

    C. _____

    D. Cozumel, Mexico

TRANSITION: *You now know which exotic places you'll be visiting. You will have a choice of many fun things to do while on shore.*

IV. Shore visit activities

    A. _____

    B. Activities for sports lovers

        1. _____

            a) Waterskiing

            b) _____

            c) _____

        2. Land sports

            a) _____

            b) _____

    C. _____

TRANSITION: *We hope the shore visit activities won't tire you out too much. You'll need your energy, because once you're back on the ship many other activities await you!*

V. _____

    A. Afternoon and evening bingo in captain's lounge

    B. _____

    C. Competitive games

        1. _____

        2. _____

    D. _____

    E. _____

TRANSITION: *With all these great onboard activities, you might not even want to leave the ship at all!*

CONCLUSION

I. I'm sure you will now agree that a Fantasia Cruise would be the perfect vacation.
    A. The guest accommodations are second to none.
    B. The ship has wonderful facilities for you to enjoy.
    C. You'll visit four unforgettable places.
    D. There are many shore visit activities.
    E. There are many things for you to do while aboard the ship.

II. Your dream vacation awaits you. Make your reservation soon and cruise to paradise with Fantasia!

Missing Headings and Supporting Ideas

Casino open twenty-four hours a day	Porthole in every cabin
Olympic-size swimming pool	Guided tours of each port
King-size bed in every cabin	Port-au-Prince, Haiti
Color TV in each cabin	Three elegant restaurants
Shipboard activities	Visits to four exotic places
Water sports	Sailing
Nightly shows in ship's nightclub	Ping-Pong tournaments
Puerto Plata, Dominican Republic	Costume party
Poolside shuffleboard tournaments	Hiking
Georgetown, Grand Cayman	Passenger talent show
Horseback riding	Shopping for native crafts
Fishing	Guest accommodations

Activity

Prepare an introduction, conclusion, and transitions for a speech.

1. Choose one of the speech outlines from the Exercise on pages 40–41 or prepare your own outline.

2. Prepare a conclusion to the speech.

3. Prepare an introduction to the speech.

4. Prepare a transition between the introduction and the body.

5. Prepare a transition between the body and the conclusion.

6. Prepare transitions between each section of the body.

SYLLABLE STRESS IN COMPOUND NOUNS

It's important to stress the correct syllables of words when speaking. Unfortunately, English does not use written accent marks the way some other languages do to tell us which syllable to stress. However, stress is usually placed on the first part of compound nouns.

 Exercise A

Practice saying the following compound nouns aloud. Be sure to stress the first part of each compound noun.

1. **bed**room
2. **ice** cream
3. **base**ball
4. **grape**fruit
5. **drug**store
6. **school**house
7. **foot**ball
8. **air**plane

9. **key**hole
10. **sun**tan
11. **stop** sign
12. **book**store
13. **suit**case
14. **doll**house
15. **light** bulb

Exercise B

Write twelve more compound nouns. Practice saying them aloud. Be sure to stress the first part of each compound noun.

1. _____
2. _____
3. _____
4. _____
5. _____
6. _____

7. _____
8. _____
9. _____
10. _____
11. _____
12. _____

Exercise C

Write ten sentences using compound nouns from Exercises A and B. Practice saying the sentences aloud. Be sure to stress the first part of each compound noun.

1. _____

2. _____

3. _____

4. _____

5. _____

6. _____

7. _____

8. _____

9. _____

10. _____

Chapter 4

Listening

Know how to listen and you will profit even from those who talk badly.
— Plutarch, Greek Historian

Nature has given to men one tongue but two ears, that we may hear from others twice as much as we speak.
— Epictetus, Ancient Philosopher

Hearing is good and speaking is good, but he who hears is a possessor of benefits.
— Ptahhotpe, Egyptian Vizier

Listening is one of the most important and frequent activities of human behavior. People spend close to fifty percent of their waking time listening, and college students spend almost ninety percent of their class time listening. Most people realize that it is important to listen carefully when teachers lecture, friends talk, parents or advisors provide information, bosses explain things, or radio commentators report the news.

Unfortunately, some listening habits prevent people from fully understanding what they hear. By knowing what these habits are, you can avoid them and become better listeners. The exercises and activities in this chapter will help you improve your ability to listen effectively in a variety of situations.

Bad Listening Habits and Their Cures

1. **Being Distracted by the Speaker's Appearance or Delivery**

   Habit: Some people don't listen to what a speaker is saying because they are concentrating on the person's speech patterns, gestures, posture, clothes, or appearance. For example, a friend of John's father was explaining how to apply for a job with his company. John was so busy admiring the man's gold watch and expensive suit that John forgot to listen to what he was being told.

   Cure: Concentrate on what the speaker is saying, not on how he or she looks or sounds. You can miss important information by thinking about a person's appearance or delivery style instead of paying attention to his or her words.

2. **Deciding the Topic Is Boring**

   Habit: Some people decide in advance that they will be bored by what the speaker is going to talk about and use this prejudice as an excuse not to listen. For example, the president of a local bank came to speak to a group of college students about inflation. Emma decided that she wasn't interested in the topic and would be bored, so she brought a newspaper to read during the banker's speech. The speaker gave excellent suggestions about fighting inflation and saving money. All of Emma's friends thought it was a great speech with much useful information. But she missed out because she wasn't listening.

Cure: Never take the attitude "I must sit through another boring talk." Even if you are not interested in the topic at first, remember some of the information could be important or interesting. Make an effort to listen for information that you could use later (e.g., in a college course, job, or conversation with friends or family). Adopt the attitude "I may as well listen since I'm already here."

3. **Faking Attention**

   Habit: Some people pretend to be listening, but their minds are on other things. They might be looking directly at the speaker and even nodding their heads in agreement when, in fact, they are actually daydreaming, thinking about their own problems, or planning what they want to say in response to the speech. The speaker thinks the listeners are polite and interested, when they are really not paying attention. For example, Margaret Lane, author of a *Reader's Digest* article entitled "Are You Really Listening?" describes how faking attention cost her a job. When interviewing her for a job on a newspaper, the editor described his winter ski trip. She wanted to impress him by talking about a camping trip in the same mountains and started planning her own adventure story. The editor suddenly asked, "What do you think of that?" Ms. Lane (not having listened to him) answered, "Sounds like fun!" The annoyed editor replied, "Fun? I just told you I was in the hospital with a broken leg."

   Cure: Don't just pretend to pay attention. Be sincere and take a real interest in the person speaking to you. If you are too busy to listen, ask the speaker if he or she can tell you later when you can really take the time to listen.

4. **Looking for Distractions**

   Habit: Some people allow themselves to be distracted by their surroundings. They might look out the window or at the wall, play with a pencil or hair clip, or observe how people in the room are dressed. For example, one student failed a math test because she wasn't listening when the teacher told the class to be prepared for a quiz the following day. She was looking at a boy with dandruff seated in front of her and thinking how ugly his hair looked.

Cure: Concentrate! Refuse to allow distractions to take your mind off the speaker. Develop the willpower to ignore them.

5. **Concentrating on Unimportant Details**

   Habit: Some people concentrate on specific details and miss the speaker's main points. For example, notice how the student missed the advisor's main points in the dialog below.

   ADVISOR: On Friday, May 10, Miss Martin, the Director of Financial Aid, spoke about applying for a scholarship.

   STUDENT: May 10 was a Thursday, not a Friday.

   ADVISOR: I'll now summarize this important information for you....

   STUDENT: It's not Miss Martin, it's Mrs. Martin.

   ADVISOR: Write to the address I gave you and send the application.

   STUDENT: What address? What application?

   Cure: When listening, pay attention to the general purpose of the message rather than to insignificant details. Listen for the main point of the talk first; then take note of any supporting facts.

6. **Reacting Emotionally to Trigger Words**

   Habit: Some people ignore or distort what a speaker is saying because they react emotionally to "trigger words"—words that cause positive or negative emotional reactions. When this happens, their ability to listen decreases because they allow their emotions to take over. For example, if a favorite subject is mentioned, some people begin thinking about it and want to express their opinions. Similarly, if an unpleasant subject is mentioned, some people get upset or angry and stop listening to what the speaker is saying.

   For example, Pilar, a student from Argentina, was listening to her economics professor discuss the economy in South America. As soon as he mentioned Buenos Aires, Pilar became homesick and started to think about her friends and family still there. The mention of Buenos Aires caused her to have a pleasant emotional reaction. However, pleasant or not, the trigger word "Buenos Aires" caused Pilar to stop listening to her teacher's lecture.

Here's another example. Several students have reported that "nuclear weapons" or "nuclear arms race" are their emotional trigger words. Upon hearing newscasters say these words, they become so preoccupied with the possibility of World War III that they stop listening to the rest of the newscast even when the commentator has started to discuss other topics.

Cure: Identify the trigger words—specific words, people, and topics—that affect you. Once you determine what they are, you can reduce their effect on you by recognizing them as soon as they are mentioned. This strategy will help you to remain objective and to concentrate on the speaker's message. Let the speaker finish what he or she is saying before you allow past memories to cause you to react emotionally.

Activity

Write your own positive and negative trigger words in the chart below. When you have finished, discuss your responses in small groups. How do your classmates react when they hear each of these words?

	Negative Trigger Words	Positive Trigger Words
Specific Words		
People		
Topics		

Exercise

Next to each example, write the letter of one of the following bad listening habits that is demonstrated:

    a. Being distracted by speaker's appearance or delivery
    b. Deciding the topic is boring
    c. Faking attention
    d. Looking for distractions
    e. Concentrating on unimportant details
    f. Reacting to emotional triggers

____ 1. A Mexican tour guide was explaining the history of Chapultepec Castle to some American tourists. One of the tourists loved to hear the way Spanish speakers roll the letter *r* and paid more attention to the guide's pronunciation than to his explanation.

____ 2. Linda was doing a crossword puzzle when her friend Rosa telephoned. As Rosa was talking, Linda kept saying "Really?" and "I see" to make Rosa think she was listening. Linda was really working on her crossword puzzle.

____ 3. Akiko's physical-education teacher was explaining how to save the life of a heart-attack victim through the use of CPR. As the teacher was speaking, Akiko was saddened by the memory of her grandfather who had recently died of a heart attack. All she could think about was the good times they had together before he died.

____ 4. Your friend is teaching you how to use his new camera. You want to learn to use the camera, but you notice he just bought an expensive stereo system with four speakers. While he is talking, you are looking at his new stereo, wishing you could afford one also.

____ 5. Nachum, an Israeli student, told us that whenever the subject of the Holocaust is mentioned, he gets very upset and emotional. He immediately thinks of his grandparents, who died in a concentration camp; he is completely unable to listen to the speaker or follow the rest of the conversation.

____ 6. A counselor was speaking about college graduation requirements. Lena decided that she didn't need to listen and would look up the information in the college catalog. She wrote a letter to her boyfriend instead of listening to the speaker. She missed valuable information about new requirements that were not printed in the catalog.

_____ 7. Your aunt is not a stylish dresser. You never really listen to what she says because, when you see her, you think about how her clothes don't match and how they look out of style.

_____ 8. A group of people were listening to a book review at their local library. One man was concentrating on remembering the exact ages and birthdays of all the book's characters; unfortunately, he missed much of the librarian's fascinating description of the novel's general plot.

Listening Exercises

Exercise 1
Listen to the following passage. Fill in the blanks with the missing *nouns*.

The heart is a powerful _____ located in the _____ directly under the _____. The heart of _____ and other _____ and of birds is divided into four _____. They are the left and right auricles and the left and right ventricles. The auricles receive _____ from the _____ and push it into the ventricles. The _____ pump the blood out of the _____ and around the _____.

Beating is an automatic _____ of the heart. It begins early in embryonic _____ before the _____ is born, and continues without stopping throughout _____. All body _____ constantly need _____, which is carried to them by the circulating _____. If a person's heart stops beating for a few _____, unconsciousness will result. _____ will occur if it stops for a few _____. A resting person's heart pumps about five _____ of blood per minute. In seventy _____, a human's _____ beats about two billion, six hundred million times. The number of _____ per minute and the amount of _____ pumped are greatly increased during _____.

The heart is able to continue beating after its _____ have been cut. In fact, if it is kept in the proper type of _____, it will beat even when entirely removed from the _____.

Exercise 2

Listen to the passage. Fill in the blanks with the missing *verbs*.

Water is the most precious of all the resources on earth. Without water, no plant, animal, or any form of life could have _____. Believe it or not, every drop of water that was on the earth when it was _____ still _____ on our planet today. Water is always _____. It has _____ around the globe many times. The heat of the sun _____ it from the oceans. It is _____ along in clouds by winds. Water _____ from the sky in the form of rain, snow, hail, or sleet. It will _____ for hundreds of years in ice caps and glaciers or _____ back to the sea through storm sewers and rivers. Almost all the water on earth is in the oceans. No one is exactly certain, but scientists _____ that life itself _____ in the sea about three billion years ago.

Exercise 3

Listen to a reading of the article "Lying: Studies in Deception." Based on the information in the reading, write *T* if the statement is *true* and *F* if the statement is *false*.

_____ 1. The ability to lie well is not a simple skill to learn.

_____ 2. An expert can easily detect a good liar.

_____ 3. Many companies and government agencies use polygraph tests each year.

_____ 4. Most experts agree that polygraph or lie-detector tests are reliable.

_____ 5. Several thousand publications contend that lie-detector tests are accurate.

_____ 6. People have only recently become interested in attempting to detect lies.

Exercise 4

Listen to a passage about daydreaming. Based on the information in the passage, write *T* if the statement is *true* and *F* if the statement is *false*.

_____ 1. Almost everyone daydreams or fantasizes daily.

_____ 2. Most daydreaming occurs in company.

_____ 3. Daydreaming is a perfectly normal and enjoyable activity.

_____ 4. Women daydream or fantasize more than men.

_____ 5. Older people tend to daydream about the past.

_____ 6. It is not normal for children to engage in fantasy play.

_____ 7. Although daydreaming has several advantages, it can be harmful.

Exercise 5

Listen to the passage. Based on the information in the passage, answer the questions below.

1. Where did the young man sit down?

   _____

2. Who started the conversation?

   _____

3. How old did the old woman feel?

   _____

4. What did the young man say?

   _____

5. Did the old woman agree with what the young man said? Why?

   _____

Exercise 6

Listen to the passage. Based on the information in the passage, answer the questions below.

1. Where did the businessman go one afternoon?

   _____

2. What was wrong with the businessman?

   _____

3. How long had the bartender known the businessman?

   _____

4. What did the bartender tell the businessman?

   _____

5. How did the businessman answer?

   _____

6. What was the bartender's final remark?

   _____

7. What is your opinion about the bartender's final statement?

   _____

Exercise 7

Listen to the passage. Based on the information in the passage, answer the questions below.

1. Who was the first person to have an umbrella?

   _____

2. What was this first umbrella made of?

   _____

3. What is the origin and meaning of the word *umbrella*?

   _____

4. When did people start using umbrellas in the rain?

_____

5. What were umbrella ribs made of in the early 1900s?

_____

6. What are umbrellas made of today?

_____

7. What kind of umbrella has not yet been invented?

_____

8. Which companies find more lost umbrellas than anything else?

_____

Exercise 8

Listen to the questions and think about them carefully before answering them below. Be sure to answer each question before you hear the next one.

1. _____

2. _____

3. _____

4. _____

5. _____

6. _____

7. _____

8. _____

9. _____

10. _____

Listen and follow the directions.

1. 2   5   17   20   24   100   59

2. red blue chair green desk table black seven twenty

3. W   B   X   E   Z   C   U

4.

5. ○   △   ☐   ☐

6. apple   pear   corn   carrot   banana   paper   squash

7. _____

8.

9. [☐☐☐]

10. _____

_____

🎧 **Exercise 10**

You will hear eight short passages, each followed by two or three statements. Based on the information in each passage, check whether the statements are fact or opinion.

Example

Richard is a popular male name. Rick, Richie, and Dick are common nicknames for boys and men named Richard.

Statement	Fact	Opinion
a) Many boys are named Richard.	✓	
b) Rick is a nicer name than Dick or Richie.		✓

Statement	Fact	Opinion		Statement	Fact	Opinion
1. a)	_____	_____		5. a)	_____	_____
b)	_____	_____		b)	_____	_____
c)	_____	_____				
2. a)	_____	_____		6. a)	_____	_____
b)	_____	_____		b)	_____	_____
c)	_____	_____				
3. a)	_____	_____		7. a)	_____	_____
b)	_____	_____		b)	_____	_____
c)	_____	_____				
4. a)	_____	_____		8. a)	_____	_____
b)	_____	_____		b)	_____	_____
				c)	_____	_____

Pronunciation Tip

[i] AND [ɪ]

Some students confuse the vowel sounds [i] (as in *bean*), and [ɪ] (as in *bin*). If they confuse these sounds, **it** sounds like **eat** and **sheep** sounds like **ship**.

The sound [i] is long and stressed. When you pronounce it, tense your lips and spread them into a smile. The sound [ɪ] is short and relaxed. When you pronounce it, don't tense your lips or move your tongue.

Exercise A

Read the following pairs of words and sentences aloud. Be sure to tense your lips and make a long sound when pronouncing words with [i]. Be sure to relax your lips and make a short sound when pronouncing words with [ɪ].

[i]	[ɪ]
1. fee**t**	fit
2. sh**ee**p	sh**i**p
3. t**ea**m	T**i**m
4. When did he sl**ee**p?	When did he sl**i**p?
5. She will l**ea**ve.	She will l**i**ve.
6. Change the wh**ee**l.	Change the w**i**ll.

Exercise B

Read the following sentences aloud. Circle the boldfaced words with the vowel sound [i] and underline those with the vowel sound [ɪ].

1. Please **sit** in the **seat**.
2. He **did** a good **deed**.
3. **Tim** made the **team**.
4. Potato **chips** are **cheap**.
5. The shoes don't **fit** my **feet**.

Exercise C

Read the dialog below silently. Circle the words with the vowel sound [i] and underline those with the vowel sound [ɪ]. Then practice reading the dialog aloud with a partner.

JIM: Hi, Tina! Do you have a minute?

TINA: Yes, Jim. What is it?

JIM: My sister is in the city on business. We are going to eat dinner out tonight. Can you recommend a place to eat?

TINA: There is a fine seafood restaurant on Fifth Street. The fish is fresh and the shrimp is great. But it isn't cheap!

JIM: That's OK. It will be "feast today, famine tomorrow!" I'll just have to eat beans for the rest of the week!

Chapter 5

Speaking to Inform

Informative speaking is all around us. Any speech is an informative speech if it presents information to an audience. A report, a teacher's explanation, and a talk at a group meeting are all examples of informative speeches.

When do we make informative speeches? We make them all the time. Whenever we give a stranger directions, explain a problem to a mechanic, or describe an illness to a doctor, we are speaking to inform.

The goal in giving an informative speech is to state ideas simply, clearly, and interestingly. If you achieve this goal, the audience will understand and remember your speech. In this chapter, you will learn how to build an informative speech.

Preparing for the Informative Speech

You build an informative speech the way you build a house. For both constructions, you first need a blueprint, a vision of what you want to build. The steps for preparing an informative speech are:

1. Analyzing your audience
2. Choosing your topic
3. Narrowing your topic
4. Gathering information
5. Preparing visual aids
6. Organizing your speech

If you follow these steps, or this blueprint, you will create an informative speech that is well-organized, interesting, and memorable.

1. Analyze the Audience
2. Choose a Topic
3. Narrow the Topic
4. Gather Information
5. Prepare Visual Aids
6. Organize the Speech

1. Analyzing Your Audience

Start preparing for your informative speech by getting as much information about your audience as you can. This information will help you prepare a speech that is relevant and interesting to your listeners. What do you need to know about your audience in order to be able to do this?

1. Analyze the Audience

Age Range

What is the age range of your audience? What topics would interest them? If they are young, an appropriate speech topic might be choosing a career. However, if they are middle-aged, a good topic might be planning for retirement.

Sex Distribution

What is the sex distribution of your audience? If there are both men and women, choose a topic that is interesting to both. On the other hand, if there are only men or only women, you can choose a topic of specific interest to that group.

Occupation(s)

Is your audience made up of college students who don't work? Or do most of your classmates have jobs? If they have jobs, where do they work? What do they do? If members of your audience have occupations in common, you could build your speech on this shared background.

Economic Level(s)

What is the financial position of your audience? You would not, for example, try to inform the average college student on how to build a sauna in your jet plane. However, it might be a great topic for a group of millionaires.

General Background

What are the general backgrounds, attitudes, and religious beliefs of your audience? It would not be appropriate, for example, to talk to vegetarians about the best steak restaurants in Buenos Aires. Similarly, people who are against smoking would probably not be interested in a speech about different types of cigars. Other questions should also be considered. Are your listeners married? Do they have children? What are their racial and ethnic backgrounds? Consider these factors in order to choose a topic that is of interest to everyone.

Be sure to avoid statements that may offend people in your audience. For example, senior citizens might not like to be called "the elderly," and women may object to being called "girls." To be on the safe side, avoid biased generalizations based on sex, occupation, economic level, or general background.

Activity

Your classmates will be your audience for most speeches. Use the form below to perform a complete analysis of your classmates. This will help you prepare your future speeches.

Analysis of Audience	
Age Range	
Sex Distribution	
Occupation(s)	
Economic Level(s)	
General Background	

2. Choosing Your Topic

2. Choose a Topic

When asked to choose a topic, your first question might be "What should I talk about?" A quick and easy way to find a good topic is to choose something that you know a lot about or that really interests you. A good topic choice is an experience that you remember vividly and are enthusiastic about.

Example A

A student who had gone for a hot-air balloon ride while on vacation in Australia spoke enthusiastically about hot-air balloons.

Example B

A student who had come to the United States from Poland at the age of eighteen gave an excellent speech about problems facing immigrants in a new country.

A topic for which you have special skills or work experience is also a good possibility.

Example

Having worked for her father, a businessman who bought and sold emeralds in Colombia, a student gave a terrific speech about emeralds.

Another option is to choose a topic that you are knowledgeable about.

Example

A student who had been collecting stamps since he was nine years old made an excellent speech about the history of the postage stamp.

The informative speeches described above were particularly good because the students chose topics they were really interested in and that they already knew something about. Think about your special interests, hobbies, or personal experiences, and you will have no trouble choosing a topic.

3. Narrowing Your Topic

The next step is to narrow your topic. If you picked a topic that you know a lot about, you probably know more about it than your audience. Although being knowledgeable is important, be careful not to tell everything you know about your topic. Doing so is a bad idea for two reasons. First of all, it

3. Narrow the Topic

is impossible to say everything there is to say about a topic in a short amount of time. If, for example, you have five minutes to talk about soccer, it is impossible to say everything about soccer in five minutes. You would only be able to go over broad generalizations about the sport. You would have to limit your talk to, for example, the history of soccer or the basic rules of soccer. Secondly, your audience cannot remember too many details after one five-minute speech. Limit your topic so that your audience can understand and remember it. For example, if your topic is Mexico City and you try to cover its history, climate, geography, social and political problems, restaurants, and museums in five minutes, your audience will never remember it all. However, they will remember more if you limit your topic to shopping in Mexico City or to popular tourist attractions there.

How do you narrow an informative speech topic effectively? It may help to remember that a good informative speech topic:

- is specific
- contains only one idea
- is achievable

Is Your Topic Specific?

Limit your topic to one particular aspect of the topic. For example, the topic "hurricanes" is too general, but the topics "preparing for hurricanes" and "dangerous effects of hurricanes" are specific.

Does Your Topic Contain Only One Idea?

Make sure your topic has just one idea. For example, the topic "choosing a hotel and buying a car in a foreign country" has two ideas, but the topics "choosing a hotel in a foreign country" and "buying a car in a foreign country" each contain one idea.

Is Your Topic Achievable?

Make sure the audience is actually able to do, understand, or remember something after your speech is over. For example, if you give a "how to" speech, like "how to weave an Oriental rug," your audience should be able to weave an Oriental rug after hearing your speech. Such a complicated task, though, is probably not achievable. However, the topic "how to buy an Oriental rug" is achievable since your audience would be able to use this information if they ever went shopping for an Oriental rug. Similarly, after hearing a speech about building a personal computer, most people would not be able to build a personal computer. However, after hearing a speech about the use of computers in education, they would be able to remember valuable information about the topic.

Activity

Indicate whether the topics that follow:

    a. are too general

    b. contain more than one idea

    c. are not achievable

    d. are good topics

Discuss your answers.

Examples

_a_ South America

_c_ How to Become a Concert Pianist

_d_ The Significance of Dreams

____ 1. Electronic Watches and Calculators

____ 2. How to Buy a Used Car

____ 3. Musical Instruments

____ 4. Writing a Résumé

____ 5. Child Abuse

____ 6. How to Fly an Airplane

____ 7. Applying for a Bank Loan

____ 8. Ecuador

____ 9. Birds

____ 10. Snakes

____ 11. Choosing and Caring for a Parrot

____ 12. Basic Techniques of Dog Training

____ 13. Life-Saving Uses of Snake Venom

____ 14. The History of Hawaii and Alaska

____ 15. The Best Way to Lose Weight

____ 16. The Galápagos Islands

____ 17. The Use of Marijuana in Medicine

____ 18. Chinese New Year Traditions

____ 19. The Celebration of Three Kings' Day in Mexico and Christmas in Germany

____ 20. How to Rebuild Your Car's Engine

4. Gathering Information

4. Gather Information

Now that you have analyzed your audience, chosen your topic, and narrowed it, you need to gather information so you can prepare the actual speech. There are two places to look for material for your speech:

- Within yourself. Write down what you already know about the topic.
- Outside yourself. Interview people who know something about your topic or do research in the library or on the Internet.

Find more information about your topic than you can use. You will then be able to choose which information to include in your speech instead of having to "stretch" your facts to fill time when you don't have enough. This extra knowledge may also be helpful if you are asked to answer questions after your presentation.

Interviews

Consult people who know something about your topic. In every college or university and in every community, experts who can help you are available. Your peers, teachers, or other people you know may also have specialized knowledge about your topic. You may decide to interview some of these people.

Before you interview anyone, decide what questions you will ask and how you will ask them. There are five basic types of questions that you can use. The types of questions and examples follow.

1. **Open-ended questions** (*or* **information questions**):

   How do you feel about the recent scandal in our city government?

   What do you think about this new "foolproof diet" on the market?

2. **Closed-ended questions** (*or* **yes/no questions**):

   Do you think the new city manager should be removed from office just because she has been indicted on corruption charges?

   Have you ever been on a diet that didn't work?

3. **Scale questions:**

   How would you rate our city government?

   Poor   Fair   Average   Good   Excellent

4. **Directive questions (specific information questions):**

   Could you give me two reasons why people fail on most diets?

5. **Multiple-choice questions:**

   How many diets do most people try in a lifetime?

   ____ None   ____ One   ____ Two to five

   ____ Six to ten   ____ Eleven to twenty   ____ Over twenty

Library and Internet Research

College and university libraries are great places to find books, magazines, newspaper articles, and journals about your topic. The *Reader's Guide to Periodical Literature* can refer you to relevant magazine articles, indexes for major newspapers (e.g., *New York Times Index*) can lead you to pertinent newspaper articles, and journals published by professional organizations (e.g., the *AMA Journal*, published by the American Medical Association) often have more specific information. Dictionaries and encyclopedias give general information about most subjects and can be useful for defining terms and concepts. Encyclopedic dictionaries may include idiomatic expressions and famous quotations that you can use in your speech as well.

Books are cited alphabetically by author, by title, and by subject. You can use the computer terminals in the library to find where books are located. If you can't find what you're looking for, ask the reference librarian. He or she is there to help.

The Internet is a great source of current information about most topics. Be sure to check the accuracy of any information you find. Make sure the source of any information you use is reliable. Also, compare the information from different Web sites.

It's helpful to record every piece of information, fact, or quotation you find on a separate four-by-six-inch note card. Include bibliographic information about your source. That way, if you need to find additional information, you will remember where you found your facts. Also, if you are asked about your sources after your speech, you will have the information at your fingertips.

5. Preparing Visual Aids

Why use visual aids? The answer is that visual aids—objects, models, pictures, charts, diagrams, and even physical demonstrations—help make a speech clear and interesting. They add variety, capture attention, illustrate concepts, and provide entertainment. Visual aids help your audience to actually see and experience what you are talking about.

5. Prepare Visual Aids

Example A

In a speech about funeral customs in Japan, this picture of an actual Japanese funeral made the speech more interesting:

Example B

In a speech about the increasing population in the United States, the following bar graph helped the students "see" and remember the statistics:

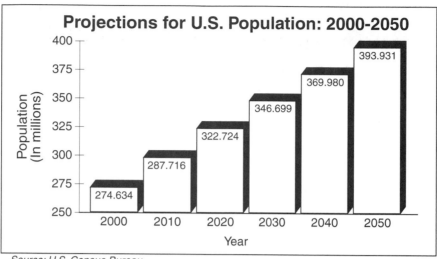

Source: U.S. Census Bureau

Example C

In a speech about asthma, a student conducted a demonstration that involved the whole class. She gave the audience drinking straws and instructed them to place the straws between their lips and to inhale and exhale through them. They were extremely uncomfortable breathing this way and felt like they would suffocate. The student explained that this is how people with asthma usually feel when attempting to breathe due to the constricting and narrowing of their tracheas. This demonstration helped the audience to "experience" the information as well as to understand and remember it long after the speech ended.

Creating and Using Visual Aids

Visual aids are helpful in three ways:
- They help the speaker get organized.
- They help the audience understand the information.
- They help the audience remember the speech.

Not only is it important to find or to create helpful visual aids, it is also important to use them effectively during your speech. The following tips can help:

1. **Use visual aids that are large enough for everyone to see.** Measure the distance (in feet) from your visual aid to the back of the room and divide it by twenty. This number—the quotient—should be the minimum letter height (in inches) of any words used in your visual aid. For example, if the last row is forty feet from your visual aid, divide forty by twenty. Your minimum letter height should be two inches.

2. **Do not pass out objects or papers during your speech.** If people are looking at objects or reading papers, they will not be listening to what you say.

3. **Keep charts, maps, and graphs very simple.** Don't try to show too many details in one visual aid.

4. **Look at your audience, not at your visual aids.** When you are showing a picture or graph, be sure to maintain eye contact with your listeners.

5. **Put your visual aids away after you have finished using them.** For example, if you are starting to speak about the Temple of Heaven in Beijing, don't leave up a picture of the Great Wall of China that was used in an earlier section of your speech.

6. **Practice using your visual aids with your speech before you actually deliver it.** Practice when, where, and how you will use them.

6. Organizing Your Speech

The next step is to organize your speech. A good informative speech includes the following components:

- Body
- Preview
- Attention-getting opener
- Summary
- Memorable concluding remarks

6. Organize the Speech

Step 1: Prepare the Body

First, prepare the body of your speech. Arrange the points of your speech in a clear, logical manner. That way, your audience can follow you, understand your information, and remember what you have said. In order to do this, it is important to choose an organizational pattern that fits your topic.

Read about the eight organizational patterns below. Then, choose the best one for your particular topic.

1. **Past-Present-Future.** Use this pattern to discuss how something once was, how it has changed, and how it will be in the future. For example, in discussing the Olympics, you might organize your information under the following three headings:

   I. The history of the Olympics

   II. The Olympics today

   III. The future of the Olympics

2. **Time.** Use this pattern to describe how processes, personal experiences, events, or activities happen by the hour, part of the day, week, month, or year. It can also be used to explain the steps in a process. For example, in speaking about making a speech, you might organize your information under the following headings:

   I. Choosing a topic

   II. Gathering information

   III. Making an outline

   IV. Presenting the speech

3. **Problem-Solution.** Use this pattern to speak about a specific problem and ways to solve it. (Note: A problem isn't always a negative situation, such as crime or child abuse. It can also be a positive situation, such as choosing a career or deciding where to go on vacation.) For example, in speaking about the problem of choosing the college that's right for you, you might present the following solutions:

   I. Read the different college catalogs.

   II. Visit campuses of different colleges.

   III. Talk to people who attend various colleges.

   IV. Talk to teachers at the colleges you are considering.

4. **Location.** Use this pattern to divide a topic into different geographical locations. For example, In speaking about interesting marriage customs, you might use the following sequence:

  I. Marriage customs in Japan
  II. Marriage customs in Saudi Arabia
  III. Marriage customs in the United States

5. **Cause-Effect.** Use this pattern to describe a particular situation and its effects. For example, in speaking about the effects of cigarette smoking, you might discuss:

  I. The effects of smoking on pregnant women
  II. The effects of secondhand smoke
  III. The effects of smoking on people with allergies

6. **Effect-Cause.** Use this pattern to describe a particular situation and its causes. For example, in speaking about reasons for drug addiction, you might discuss:

  I. The easy availability of drugs
  II. The need to escape from the pressures of work
  III. The lack of education about harmful effects of drugs

7. **Related Subtopics.** Use this pattern to divide one topic into different parts, or subtopics. For example, in speaking about false advertising, you might discuss:

  I. False advertising on television
  II. False advertising in magazines
  III. False advertising on the radio

8. **Advantage-Disadvantage.** Use this pattern to talk about both positive and negative aspects of a topic in a balanced, objective manner. For example, in speaking about the death penalty, you might discuss:

  I. Advantages of capital punishment
  II. Disadvantages of capital punishment

Activity

To the left of each item, write the letter of the organizational pattern used.

a. Past-Present-Future   e. Cause-Effect
b. Time   f. Effect-Cause
c. Problem-Solution   g. Related Subtopics
d. Location   h. Advantage-Disadvantage

Examples

__c__ In a speech about high school dropouts, Mary presented a series of suggestions for parents and teachers to follow in order to help teenagers do well in high school. She also suggested that students should help and encourage each other to graduate from high school.

__f__ José also spoke about high school dropouts. He discussed some reasons why students drop out of school. He pointed out that some students don't receive encouragement at home, while others need money to help support their families so they leave school to get jobs. Also, some would rather "hang out" with friends than go to class.

____ 1. In Kim's speech about looking for a job, he explained that the first thing to do is to prepare a résumé. The second thing to do is to read the employment section in the newspaper or to visit an employment agency. Kim said the last thing to do is to schedule job interviews and pray a lot.

____ 2. In Michelle's speech about gambling, she chose three states in which certain types of gambling are legal—Florida, New York, and Nevada. She then described the different forms of gambling permissible in each state.

____ 3. In a speech about automobiles, Jean described cars of sixty years ago and how hard they were to drive. She then talked about the automatic cars we have today with their many modern features. Finally, she said that some day cars would be driven by computers so that the "drivers" can relax and enjoy the ride.

____ 4. In a speech about saving money, Hector said that saving money is a problem because most products are very expensive. He suggested that some good ways to save money are to comparison shop for the best prices, buy things on sale, and eat less expensive foods.

_____ 5. In a speech about a day in the life of a teacher, Luisa talked about early-morning preparation, classroom teaching, and after-school activities.

_____ 6. In a speech about entertainment in his city, Claude talked about entertainment for music lovers, entertainment for art lovers, and entertainment for theater lovers.

_____ 7. In a speech about pets, Kimiko spoke about the problems people have with pets as well as the joy pets can give their owners.

_____ 8. In a speech about depression, Leonardo described the disorder and many of its symptoms. He then discussed how drugs and psychological counseling are used to treat depression.

_____ 9. In a speech about obesity in the United States, Nancy talked about its characteristics. She said that people are obese because they don't exercise, they don't eat right, and they lack the motivation to go on diets.

_____ 10. In a speech about diamonds, Antoine stated that diamonds are classified by the three C's: cut, color, and clarity. He then explained each of these characteristics in more detail.

Step 2: Prepare a Preview

After deciding on an organizational pattern and determining the main headings in the body of your speech, you next need to prepare a preview. You should tell your audience what you're going to cover before you actually begin the body of your speech. This should be easy because you have already determined what you will cover in your headings.

Example A

My purpose today is to tell you what to do in the event of a hurricane. I will cover three major areas:

    A. First, how to prepare for a hurricane

    B. Second, what safety measures to take during a hurricane

    C. Third, what to do after the storm is over

Example B

In discussing left-handed people, I will explain three interesting facts:

    A. First, I'll explain why left-handed people have more accidents than other people.

    B. Second, I'll inform you about the four most common problems that left-handed people face.

    C. Third, I'll tell you about some world-famous "lefties."

In each example, the speaker clearly stated the purpose and numbered the subpoints. The audience thus knows exactly what the speaker is going to discuss.

Step 3: Prepare an Attention-Getting Opener

At the beginning of your speech, it is very important to grab your audience's attention and make them interested in what you have to say. Four different ways to prepare an interesting, attention-getting introduction follow:

1. **Ask your audience a series of rhetorical questions**. Rhetorical questions are asked for dramatic effect with no answers expected. Your listeners will immediately be interested in knowing the answers. The following rhetorical questions were used to open a speech about the process of getting a tattoo:

   What can cost ten dollars or a thousand dollars?
   What can be every color of the rainbow?
   What can be with you as long as you live?
   What can you wear on your arm, your cheek, your leg, or even your back?

2. **Tell a story.** People love to listen to a story. They want to find out what it is about. This story was used to open a speech about the Gold Museum in Bogotá, Colombia:

   A guard took me into a square room with no lights. The room was so black I couldn't even see my own feet. All of a sudden a hidden electric wall closed behind me. There was no way out. I thought I was in a tomb. All at once bright lights came on. I was surrounded by gold on all four sides!

3. **State a surprising fact.** The statement below was used to introduce a speech about the billion-dollar business of bartering. The speaker talked about ways to trade skills, services, or products to get almost anything you want without cash:

   You can get almost anything you want without cash! And you can begin today!

4. **State a well-known quotation.** This quotation from William Shakespeare's *Hamlet* was used to open a speech about the disadvantages of borrowing:

   Neither a borrower nor a lender be, for loan oft loses both itself and friend.

Step 4: Prepare a Summary

Every speech needs a summary of the information presented. The best way to summarize your information is to remind your audience of what you said by repeating the main points covered in the body of your speech.

Example A

Well, I've given you some very important information today. You now know:

    A. How to prepare if a hurricane is coming

    B. What safety measures to take during the storm

    C. What to do after the hurricane is over

Example B

As you can see, the Olympic Games are very important to people all over the world. I hope you learned some interesting information about:

    A. The history of the Olympics

    B. The Olympics today

    C. The future of the Olympic Games

Step 5: Prepare Memorable Concluding Remarks

Every speech needs an ending that leaves the audience thinking about and remembering what was said. Like attention-getting openers, memorable concluding remarks can take the form of rhetorical questions, stories, surprising facts, or quotations. Of these suggestions, quotations are popular among many famous public speakers:

Example A

President John F. Kennedy ended many of his speeches with this quotation from the poet Robert Browning: "Some men see things as they are, and ask, 'Why?' I dare to dream of things that never were, and ask, 'Why not?'"

Example B

Civil-rights leader Martin Luther King Jr. ended his famous "I Have a Dream" speech with words from an old spiritual song: "Free at last, free at last, thank God Almighty, we are free at last."

Say your memorable concluding remarks slowly and clearly, maintaining eye contact with your audience. Be as dramatic and confident as possible!

Outlining an Informative Speech

The outline that follows shows how one student outlined an informative speech. Notice how it includes the following components:

- Attention-getting opener
- Preview
- Body
- Summary
- Memorable concluding remarks

Also, notice how transitions have been used to connect the components.

ATTENTION-GETTING OPENER

Every student in this room has something in common with famous astronauts, Olympic athletes, actors, politicians, and business executives. It's a common affliction that causes pain, suffering, and distress. Can you guess what it is? I'll tell you. It's called stage fright.

PREVIEW

Today we will be learning four major facts about stage fright.

   I. The physical symptoms of stage fright

  II. The causes of stage fright

 III. Famous people who have had stage fright

 IV. What can be done about stage fright

TRANSITION: *OK, let's get started on our investigation of stage fright by first looking at its six major symptoms.*

BODY

   I. Physical symptoms of stage fright

     A. Rapid breathing

     B. Rapid heart rate

     C. Dry mouth

     D. Butterflies in stomach

     E. Increased perspiration

     F. Trembling hands

TRANSITION: *Now you understand the symptoms of stage fright. Let's continue our investigation by examining the causes of stage fright.*

II. Causes of stage fright
   A. Many people worry that they'll forget what they want to say.
   B. Others are afraid that they'll look silly.
   C. Some people think that the audience won't like them.
   D. International students might worry that their English isn't very good.

TRANSITION: *Now you are aware of some of the causes of stage fright. Let's continue our inquiry into stage fright by looking at a few famous people who have suffered from this affliction.*

III. Famous people who have had stage fright
   A. Winston Churchill once said that he thought there was a block of ice in his stomach each time he made a speech.
   B. Julio Iglesias has revealed that he is nervous about his pronunciation when speaking English.
   C. Jane Fonda has admitted to having "tremendous fear."
   D. Olivia Newton-John admits to shaking and crying before a performance.

TRANSITION: *As you can see, you are in good company with famous people who have had stage fright. Now, let's investigate what you can do to overcome this common problem.*

IV. Solutions for stage fright
   A. Short-term solutions
      1. Be thoroughly prepared and practice before a presentation.
      2. Take your time before you start to speak.
         a) Gently put your notes on the speaker's stand.
         b) Establish eye contact with your audience before beginning.
         c) Take several deep breaths before beginning.
   B. Long-term solutions
      1. Remember that stage fright is normal.
      2. Get as much experience as possible.
      3. Talk about stage fright with friends.

TRANSITION: *Now that you understand what you can do to reduce stage fright, our investigation is complete.*

SUMMARY

You should now understand four important facts about stage fright.

    I.   The physical symptoms of stage fright

   II.   The causes of stage fright

  III.   Famous people who have had stage fright

  IV.   What can be done about stage fright

MEMORABLE CONCLUDING REMARKS

In conclusion, stage fright is like a lion in a cage. It's only dangerous if it's allowed to roam free! Now that you know how to deal with stage fright, you'll be able to keep this beast under control. Remember, as long as you are in control of it, your stage fright, like the lion, will be unable to harm you!

Assignment

Make an informative speech.

1. Using the Informative Speech Preparation Worksheet and Checklist on pages 85–86, prepare notes for your presentation.

2. Using the guidelines from Chapter 3: Putting Your Speech Together, outline your speech.

3. Your teacher may use the form on page 190 to evaluate your speech. Look it over so you know exactly how you will be evaluated.

4. Give a four to five minute informative speech.

Informative Speech Preparation Worksheet

1. Choose three topics that interest you.
    a) _____
    b) _____
    c) _____

2. Narrow each topic.
    a) _____
    b) _____
    c) _____

3. Choose the topic that interests you the most. Divide it into three or four subtopics.
    a) _____
    b) _____
    c) _____
    d) _____

4. Prepare an attention-getting opener.
    _____
    _____
    _____

5. Prepare a preview.
    _____
    _____
    _____

6. Prepare a summary.
    _____
    _____
    _____

7. Prepare memorable concluding remarks.
    _____
    _____
    _____

You may want to use the checklist below. Check off each step as you prepare for your speech.

Informative Speech Preparation Checklist

Name: _____   Topic: _____

Due Date: _____

____ Chose narrow, specific, achievable topic.

____ Consulted outside sources:

    ____ Interviews   ____ Books   ____ Magazines

    ____ Newspapers   ____ Dictionaries   ____ Encyclopedias

    ____ Encyclopedic dictionaries   ____ Professional journals

    ____ Internet

____ Chose organizational pattern.

____ Prepared outline.

____ Prepared body.

____ Prepared preview.

____ Prepared attention-getting opener.

____ Prepared summary.

____ Prepared memorable concluding remarks.

____ Prepared transition after introduction.

____ Prepared transition before summary.

____ Prepared transitions in body.

____ Prepared visual aids:

    ____ Objects   ____ Charts and diagrams   ____ Demonstrations

____ Practiced speech with visual aids at least three times.

[ð] AND [d]

English is one of the few languages in which the [ð] sound (as in *the*), is consistently heard. A common error is to pronounce the sound [d] instead of [ð]. If you substitute [d] for [ð], **they** sounds like **day** and **those** sounds like **doze**.

Pronounce [ð] by placing your tongue between your teeth. Pronounce [d] by placing your tongue behind them. Look in a mirror and make sure you can see the tip of your tongue as you pronounce [ð].

Exercise A

Read the following words aloud. Be sure you can feel the tip of your tongue protrude between your teeth when you pronounce [ð].

1.	**th**ey	9.	bro**th**er
2.	**th**en	10.	ei**th**er
3.	**th**at	11.	ba**th**e
4.	**th**ose	12.	smoo**th**
5.	**th**ere	13.	clo**th**e
6.	o**th**er	14.	soo**th**e
7.	mo**th**er	15.	brea**th**e
8.	fa**th**er		

Exercise B

Read the following pairs of words aloud. Be sure to place your tongue between your teeth for [ð] and behind your teeth for [d].

	[ð]	[d]
1.	**th**ey	**d**ay
2.	**th**en	**d**en
3.	**th**ere	**d**are
4.	brea**th**e	bree**d**
5.	la**th**er	la**dd**er

Exercise C

Read the following phrases and sentences aloud. Be sure to place your tongue between your teeth for [ð] in each of the boldfaced words.

1. a) **mother** and **father**
   b) **This** is my **mother** and **father**.

2. a) **other brother**
   b) Will your **other brother** be **there**?

3. a) get **together**
   b) Let's get **together another** day.

4. a) **bathe the** baby
   b) **Grandmother** must **bathe the** baby.

5. a) **than the other**
   b) **This** is better **than the other** one.

Persuasive speaking is all around us. Any speech is persuasive if its purpose is to convince others to change their feelings, beliefs, or behavior. A salesperson trying to convince someone to buy a product, a political leader trying to get someone to vote a certain way, and a teacher lecturing about why a history class should be required are all speaking to persuade.

When do we make persuasive speeches? We make them all the time. When we ask a friend to lend us money, ask our teacher for a higher grade, try to convince a sibling to lose some weight, or try to persuade a parent to buy us something, our goal is to try to change or influence others.

In this chapter, you will learn how to build a persuasive speech.

Warm Up

1. Find a partner.

2. Choose one of the persuasive-speaking situations below (or a different persuasive-speaking situation).
   - Convince your parents to let you go on a camping trip with friends.
   - Convince your younger brother (or sister) to do his (or her) homework.
   - Convince a friend that watching TV is (or isn't) a waste of time.
   - Convince your boss to give you a promotion.
   - Convince your parents that you are too young to get married.
   - Convince your teacher that you did not get help writing a composition.
   - Convince students to vote for you to be president of the senior class.
   - Convince a friend to smoke less.
   - Convince a sales clerk to let you return something you bought.
   - Convince your parents to let you get a part-time job.

3. Role-play the situation.

4. Speak persuasively about the topic for two or three minutes. Be sure to give as many reasons as possible.

Preparing for the Persuasive Speech

As with the informative speech, you build a persuasive speech step-by-step. The persuasive speech blueprint below will help you create persuasive presentations that are interesting and effective.

The steps for preparing a persuasive speech are:

1. Determining your specific purpose

2. Choosing your topic

3. Analyzing your audience

4. Gathering information

5. Preparing visual aids

6. Organizing your speech

1. Determine the Specific Purpose

2. Choose a Topic

3. Analyze the Audience

4. Gather Information

5. Prepare Visual Aids

6. Organize the Speech

1. Determining Your Specific Purpose

The general goal of persuasive speaking is to convince your listeners to change something. The first step is to decide what you want them to change—a belief, an opinion, or their behavior.

1. Determine the Specific Purpose

To Change Audience's Belief (That Something Is True or False)

In this case, your specific purpose is to convince the audience of one of the following:

- a reported fact is either true or false
- something will or won't happen
- an event was represented accurately or inaccurately

Examples

Mexico City (or Tokyo) is the largest city in the world.

The defendant committed (or did not commit) the crime.

Capital punishment is (or is not) a deterrent to crime.

There is (or is not) life after death.

To Change Audience's Opinion (About Something's Value)

In this case, your specific purpose is to convince the audience that something is one of the following:

- good or bad
- important or unimportant
- fair or unfair
- better or worse (than something else)
- helpful or not helpful

Examples

It is fair (or unfair) for foreign students to pay higher tuition.

Required courses in college are important (or unimportant).

Dogs make better (or worse) pets than cats.

New York is more (or less) interesting than San Francisco.

To Change Audience's Behavior

In this case, your specific purpose is to convince your listeners to either:

- do something they are not doing now
- stop some behavior they currently practice

Examples

You should donate blood for the campus blood drive.

You should stop drinking coffee.

You should watch TV for a maximum of one hour daily.

You should learn to scuba dive for a hobby.

Activity

Write the letter of the specific purpose next to each persuasive speech topic.

    a. Change audience's belief (that something is true or false)

    b. Change audience's opinion (about something's value)

    c. Change audience's behavior

____ 1. Everyone should learn to give artificial respiration.

____ 2. Airplane travel is the safest way to travel in the U.S.

____ 3. Soccer is a more exciting sport than baseball.

____ 4. The government should prohibit all cigarette advertising.

____ 5. Lower highway speed limits save lives.

____ 6. Single parents should be allowed to adopt children.

____ 7. History is a more important subject than biology.

____ 8. You should donate at least fifty dollars a year to your favorite charity.

____ 9. Alcoholic beverages should not be sold on Sunday.

____ 10. Parrots make wonderful pets.

2. Choosing Your Topic

2. Choose a Topic

As with your previous speeches, your first question may be "What should I talk about?" Several suggestions about how to choose appropriate topics for your persuasive speech follow.

Choose a topic that really interests you.

It is easy to think of ideas if you choose a topic that you feel strongly about.

Example A

A student who had been in a serious car accident and suffered only minor injuries because he was wearing a seat belt gave a speech entitled "The Use of Seat Belts in Cars Should Be Required by Law."

Example B

A student who had a brown belt in karate gave a speech entitled "Everyone Should Learn Karate as a Form of Self-Defense."

Suggest a change that isn't too large.

It is much easier to convince an audience to change their opinions, feelings, or behavior a little than to persuade them to change their minds completely.

Example A

It would be very difficult to convince a heavy smoker to stop smoking completely. However, you might be able to persuade him or her to cut down to one pack a day.

Example B

It would be unrealistic to try to persuade a very religious person to convert to a different faith. However, you might be able to convince him or her to read a book about different religious customs.

Choose a topic that is controversial.

Do not choose a point of view that most people already agree with.

Example A

"Exercise Is Good for You" is not a good topic. Most people already agree with this statement. However, "Jogging Is Healthier than Swimming" or "Everyone Should Enroll in an Exercise Class" are topics that are controversial since not all people agree with these claims.

Example B

The topic "English Is Spoken All Over the World" is not controversial. However, the topic "Everyone Should Learn English as a Second Language" and "English Should Be Required in South American Schools" are topics that could be argued since many people might not agree with these opinions.

Activity

Write three persuasive speech topics that you might like to use. Several general topics are listed below. What are your views about these topics? If you have a strong opinion about one, that may be a good topic for your persuasive speech.

Abortion	Separation of church and state
Racial equality	College entrance requirements
Prostitution	Legalization of marijuana
Capital punishment	Boycotting the Olympic Games
Arranged marriages	Opportunities for the handicapped
Nuclear weapons	Smoking in public places
Gun control	Living together before marriage
Donating money to charity	The legal drinking age
Working mothers	Punishment for dishonesty
Drunken drivers	Mercy killing
Animal experimentation	Violence on TV
Pornography	Highway speed limits
Women's rights	Required college courses
Sex education	Students evaluating teachers

Possible Persuasive Speech Topics:

1. _____

2. _____

3. _____

3. Analyzing Your Audience

Audience analysis was briefly discussed in Chapter 5: Speaking to Inform. Audience analysis is especially important in persuasive speaking. It is necessary to learn as much as possible about your audience's feelings and opinions toward your topic. You need to know how they feel and why they feel a certain way in order to prepare an effective persuasive speech.

3. Analyze the Audience

You can expect your listeners to feel one of three ways about the topic you choose for your persuasive speech:

Agree completely: If your audience already agrees with your belief or point of view, you must choose a different topic for your speech.

Be indifferent: If your audience doesn't care about your topic, you must find out why they are indifferent to it. In your speech, you need to:

- interest them in your topic
- convince them that it is important
- persuade them to adopt your opinion

Disagree completely: If your audience does not agree with your point of view, they probably have definite reasons for feeling the way they do. You must find out why they disagree with your opinion in order to convince them that their reasons are not good.

Activity

Choose one persuasive speech topic. Interview your classmates to find out what they think about the topic. Use the opinion survey form below to record your findings.

Opinion Survey Form

Topic: _____

General audience reaction to topic (check one):

❑ **Strongly disagree** ❑ **Disagree** ❑ **Indifferent** ❑ **Agree** ❑ **Strongly agree**

If your classmates are indifferent, it is because (check all reasons given):

❑ **They don't think your topic is important.**

❑ **They don't think your topic affects them.**

❑ **They have never heard of your topic.**

❑ **They have never given your topic any thought.**

❑ **Other:** _____

If your classmates disagree with your opinion, it is because (write all reasons given):

1. _____

2. _____

3. _____

4. _____

5. _____

4. Gathering Information

4. Gather Information

Before you begin to organize your material, you must first collect it. A good way to begin this task is to write down what you already know about your topic. Start by thinking about your own observations or experiences that relate to the point you wish to make. Once you've done this, you're ready to gather additional information necessary for an effective presentation.

As for an informative speech, you can get this information by conducting library or Internet research. Specific suggestions on how to do this are on page 72 of Chapter 5: Speaking to Inform.

Interviewing experts who have an interest in your topic can also be helpful. They may have specific data that supports your opinion.

Example A

A student's persuasive topic was "The College Should Increase the School Library's Budget." She called the head librarian, who felt the library needed additional books, better computers, more staff, and longer hours to better serve the students' needs.

Example B

Another student tried to convince the class that more scholarships should be available for international students. He interviewed the financial-aid director at the university. The director agreed with him and provided specific information about the limited funds available to help international students with their education.

When looking for information for a persuasive speech, the editorial pages of newspapers can be especially useful. They often include articles and letters that express different opinions about current controversial topics. You can also research your topic on the Internet. Often, there are links to Web sites in which different opinions about the topic are expressed.

Whenever you quote specific people or use information from newspapers, magazines, books, or the Internet in your speech, be sure to tell your audience the source of your information. This will make your evidence and arguments more believable and impress your listeners.

5. Preparing Visual Aids

Visual aids—pictures, graphs, or objects—can make your speech more interesting and can be very powerful persuasive tools. An audience is more likely to be convinced if they can actually see the importance of what you are describing.

5. Prepare Visual Aids

Example A

In a speech to persuade a class to donate money to a charity that helps children with disabilities, this picture affected the audience emotionally and, thus, made them want to make a donation:

Example B

In a speech to persuade a class to pay off the balance on their credit cards and stop using them, one student explained that Americans are declaring bankruptcy more now than at any time in history, largely because of the misuse of credit cards. He then showed the following pie chart to illustrate the high percentage of Americans that carry credit-card debt:

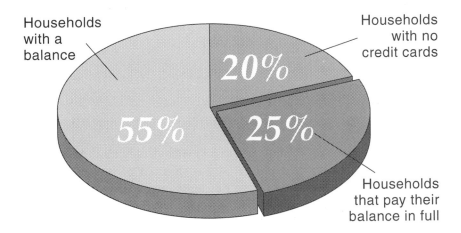

Example C

In a speech to persuade a class to complain to university officials about the polluted lakes on campus, one student held up a large bottle of dirty brown water with a dead fish in it. He explained that the dead fish came from one of the nearby lakes. This convinced the students that his speech presented a serious problem.

6. Organizing Your Speech

The next step is to organize your speech. A good persuasive speech includes the following components:

- Opener building on areas of agreement
- Statement of purpose
- Body
- Summary
- Memorable concluding remarks

6. Organize the Speech

Step 1: Prepare an Opener Building on Areas of Agreement

The introduction to a persuasive speech is very important. In order to convince listeners to agree with you, it is essential to first make them trust you and to see you as a person who thinks as they do. The best way to do this is to begin your speech by talking about common areas of agreement. You can do this by first discussing:

- common goals (we all want the same basic things in life)
- common problems (we are all concerned about this particular problem)
- common experiences (we all know what it is like to ...)

Example A: "Highway Speed Limits Are Too High"

Most of us know people who have had friends or family injured or killed in terrible car accidents on the highways. Certainly we've all read or heard about these tragedies in the news. We all want to live long, happy, healthy lives and not worry about the possibility of accidents. No one wants to worry about whether they will arrive at their destination safely every time they get in a car.

Example B: "Capital Punishment Should Be Legal"

I'm sure everyone here is concerned about crime in our community. Many of us know that it isn't always safe to go out alone at night or even to walk through a dark parking lot to get to our car. All of us want to feel safe in our homes, in our cars, and on the streets. We would all like to see the amount of crime reduced.

Example C: "Donate Money to the Red Cross"

Although we take many things for granted, we all know how fortunate we are to have nice clothes to wear, a place to live, and plenty of food to eat. We all realize that many people in the world aren't so lucky. There are many starving and homeless people on every continent. Most of you would be willing to help people less fortunate than yourselves if you knew what to do.

Step 2: Prepare a Statement of Purpose

Now that you have shown your audience that you are a sensible person who shares their values and beliefs, the next step is to clearly state the specific purpose of your speech.

Example A: "Highway Speed Limits Are Too High"

The maximum speed limit on U.S. highways should be fifty miles per hour.

Example B: "Capital Punishment Should Be Legal"
Legalizing capital punishment can help prevent crime.

Example C: "Donate Money to the Red Cross"
Everyone in this class should donate five dollars to the Red Cross.

Step 3: Prepare the Body

Now that your listeners know your specific purpose, the next step is to present evidence that will convince them to agree with you. Your audience analysis can help at this stage. Review your opinion survey form before deciding how to convince indifferent or hostile listeners.

Often, people are indifferent about a topic because they do not see how it relates to them. In order to persuade listeners with this attitude, you must convince them that your topic is interesting, important, and relevant to them.

Example A

One student wanted to persuade the class to buy water-purification systems. According to this speaker's opinion survey, his classmates were indifferent to this topic because they had never given it any thought and didn't believe it was important. However, he found a newspaper story claiming that the quality of water in their community was the worst in the United States. In the article, doctors warned that drinking this water could increase the risk of contracting cancer.

Example B

One student gave a speech entitled "Casino Gambling Should Be Legal in Miami." After doing her audience analysis, she found that her classmates were indifferent to her topic for several reasons. Some students said they don't gamble, while some international students said they will only live in Miami for a couple of years. The speaker explained that casino gambling would help the city's finances, so a proposed sales tax increase would not be necessary. If the sales tax weren't increased, prices in all stores and restaurants would be lower. Then, everyone (gamblers and nongamblers, permanent residents, and students on temporary visas) would benefit.

Hostile listeners are those who completely disagree with your opinion or belief. In order to persuade such listeners, you need to learn their reasons for disagreeing with you and convince them that these reasons are not valid.

Example A

One student wanted to persuade the class to donate blood to a hospital blood bank. According to this student's audience analysis, there were two reasons why his classmates didn't want to be blood donors.

One reason was that they were afraid of catching a disease from a dirty hypodermic needle. *To refute this reason*, the student interviewed the nurse in charge of the hospital blood bank, who explained that individually wrapped and sterilized needles are used for every blood donor and thrown away after each use. Therefore, it is impossible to catch a disease from a dirty needle.

Another reason was that some students didn't have cars and thought it was too much trouble to get to the hospital. *To refute this reason*, the speaker explained that it is very easy to get to the hospital because a bus goes from campus directly to the hospital every fifteen minutes, and the hospital offers a free transportation service to all blood donors.

Example B

One student gave a speech entitled "Capital Punishment Should Be Legal throughout the United States." This student's audience analysis showed that his classmates strongly disagreed with his claim for several reasons.

One reason was that some believed that capital punishment does not reduce crime. *To refute this reason*, the student presented evidence that there are fewer murders committed in states that have the death penalty than in states that do not and also quoted a law enforcement expert who stated that criminals are less likely to commit murder if they fear the death penalty.

One reason was that some audience members believed that murderers should be rehabilitated. *To refute this reason*, the student found results of studies showing the ineffectiveness of attempts to rehabilitate criminals. He also reported on specific studies that showed that most lawbreakers released from jail after participating in rehabilitation programs continue to commit the same crimes.

Another reason was that some audience members felt that life imprisonment is more humane than the death penalty. *To refute this reason*, the student found a report in which prisoners claimed that the thought of spending the rest of their lives in jail was unbearable. In fact, they would rather receive the death penalty.

Step 4: Prepare a Summary

An effective persuasive speech includes a summary of the evidence presented. This will remind your audience of why they should agree with you. The examples below show how evidence was summarized in two speeches.

Example A: "Donate Blood to a Hospital Blood Bank"

I'm sure you now realize that you should donate blood.

   I. It's rewarding and worthwhile.
- A. Think of a dying person whose life you might save.
- B. Think of the great personal satisfaction you'll have.

  II. It's perfectly safe and painless.
- A. Donating blood doesn't hurt a bit.
- B. There is no chance of catching any kind of disease.

 III. It's very convenient.
- A. It will only take a few minutes of your time.
- B. Free round-trip transportation to the hospital is available.

Example B: "Casino Gambling Should Be Legal in Miami"

As you can now see, legalizing casino gambling in Miami would greatly benefit you and all residents of the city.

  I. A proposed sales tax increase will not be necessary.
- A. This will keep prices you pay in restaurants lower.
- B. This will keep prices you pay in retail stores lower.

 II. Miami's finances will improve.
- A. More money will be spent to improve the roads you use.
- B. More money will be spent to improve the public parks and beaches you enjoy.
- C. More money will be spent on educational materials for children in public schools.

Step 5: Prepare Memorable Concluding Remarks

The last part of your speech to prepare is the conclusion. The conclusion of a persuasive speech should remind the audience why they should change a belief, opinion, or behavior. An effective way to do this is to make them think about the future and to remind them that the best way to redirect the future is to take some type of action.

Example A

You might be healthy now, but think about your health in a few months or in several years. We all know that the water in this city can kill us! With a home purification system, you'll never worry about drinking polluted water again. For less than seventy-five dollars, turn your kitchen faucet into an ocean of fresh water. Buy a water purification system for your sink today!

Example B

Be the best you can be! Just think—in a few short weeks a beautiful, slender, athletic body can be yours. Heads will turn as you walk down the street. Be sure to make an appointment at your local health club right away!

Outlining a Persuasive Speech

The outline thjat follows shows how one student outlined a persuasive speech. Notice how it includes the following components:

- Opener building on areas of agreement
- Statement of purpose
- Body
- Summary
- Memorable concluding remarks

Also, notice how transitions have been used to connect the components.

OPENER BUILDING ON AREAS OF AGREEMENT

Have you ever wanted to go on vacation somewhere exciting but worried that it would cost too much or that you might be bored once you got there? We all have these concerns when planning a vacation.

We all want adventure, excitement, great food, and nice hotels without spending a lot of money!

STATEMENT OF PURPOSE

Plan a trip to Chengde, China, for your next vacation!

TRANSITION: *Many of you may be worried that such a vacation will cost too much. You will be amazed to learn this is not the case.*

BODY

I. A trip to Chendge, China, is very inexpensive.

   A. Many airlines offer off-season discounts.

   B. The best hotel costs twenty-five dollars a night for a double room.

   C. You can eat three delicious meals a day for less then five dollars.

   D. Local transportation is extremely inexpensive.

      1. A rickshaw anywhere in the city costs fifteen cents.

      2. You can rent a bicycle for pennies a day.

TRANSITION: *You might think that Chengde is ugly and you'll be bored there. Let me assure you that this is not the case.*

II. There are many things to see and do in Chengde.

   A. See the most beautiful and unusual temples in the world.

      1. The Lamaist Temple of Universal Tranquility

         a) It was built by Emperor Qian Long in the eighteenth century.

         b) It has the largest wooden image of the Buddhist Goddess of Mercy, Guanyin.

      2. The Temple of Universal Joy

         a) It was built in 1766.

         b) It has an incredible double terrace.

         c) It has a fabulous double roof of yellow tiles.

      3. The eighteenth-century Temple of Universal Love

   B. Photograph the most beautiful gardens in China.

   C. Rent a rowboat and ride on one of Chengde's magnificent lakes.

   D. Go on a shopping spree.

      1. Visit a unique shop or department store.

      2. Chengde is famous for several products.

         a) Silk

         b) Furs

         c) Wood carvings

         d) Handmade Oriental rugs

TRANSITION: *Some people fear getting ill and not finding a doctor if they travel to a small city in China. This should not be a concern either.*

III. Medical care in China is excellent.
   A. Chinese hospitals and doctors provide excellent care.
   B. There are many local clinics in all cities.
   C. A variety of medicines are available.
      1. Standard antibiotics
      2. Herbal medicines

SUMMARY

I hope I've convinced you to make your next vacation Chengde, China. Remember:

I. Chengde is a very inexpensive place to visit.
II. You'll never get bored because there is so much to see and do.
III. In the unlikely event you need it, excellent medical care is available.

MEMORABLE CONCLUDING REMARKS

You can stand on the same spot where China's most powerful emperors have stood. Your eyes will see the same green mountains they saw. The spectacular scenery, cool breezes, and striking sounds will amaze you. You will find your trip was worth the time and money you spent to get there. So, see your travel agent and make plans to visit Chengde, China, soon!

Assignment

Make a persuasive speech.

1. Using the Persuasive Speech Preparation Worksheet and Checklist on pages 107–109, prepare notes for your presentation.

2. Using the guidelines from Chapter 3: Putting Your Speech Together, outline your speech.

3. Your teacher may use the form on page 191 to evaluate your speech. Look it over so you know exactly how you will be evaluated.

4. Give a four to five minute persuasive speech.

Persuasive Speech Preparation Worksheet

1. Choose three controversial topics that interest you.

   a) _____

   b) _____

   c) _____

2. Determine your purpose for speaking about each of the topics above.

   a) _____

   b) _____

   c) _____

3. Formulate a specific statement of purpose for each of the topics above.

   a) _____

   b) _____

   c) _____

4. Choose one topic, purpose, and specific persuasive claim.

   Topic _____

   Purpose _____

   Specific persuasive claim _____

5. Write three reasons why people might be indifferent or opposed to your topic.

   a) _____

   b) _____

   c) _____

   (Continued)

6. Prepare an opener building on areas of agreement.

_____

_____

_____

_____

7. State your persuasive claim.

_____

_____

8. Write the main points of the body.

_____

_____

_____

_____

9. Prepare a summary.

_____

_____

_____

_____

10. Prepare memorable concluding remarks.

_____

_____

_____

_____

You may want to use the checklist below. Check off each step as you prepare for your speech.

Persuasive Speech Preparation Checklist

Name: _____   Topic: _____

Due Date: _____

____ Chose topic about which the audience is indifferent or opposed.

____ Consulted outside sources:

    ____ Interviews   ____ Books   ____ Magazines

    ____ Newspapers   ____ Dictionaries   ____ Encyclopedias

    ____ Encyclopedic dictionaries   ____ Professional journals

    ____ Internet

____ Prepared opener building on areas of agreement.

____ Wrote statement of purpose.

____ Prepared outline for body.

____ Prepared summary.

____ Prepared memorable concluding remarks.

____ Prepared transition after introduction.

____ Prepared transition before summary.

____ Prepared transitions within body.

____ Prepared visual aids:

    ____ Objects   ____ Charts and diagrams   ____ Demonstrations

____ Practiced speech with visual aids at least three times.

STRESS IN NOUN/VERB PAIRS

In English, many two-syllable nouns and verbs are spelled alike. However, when spoken, they are pronounced differently. Most two-syllable nouns are stressed on the first syllable. Most two-syllable verbs are stressed on the second syllable.

Exercise A

Practice reading the following pairs of nouns and verbs aloud. Be sure to stress the first syllable of the noun and the second syllable of the verb.

Nouns	Verbs
1. **pre**sent (a gift)	pre**sent** (to give; to show)
2. **pro**ject (an assignment)	pro**ject** (to predict)
3. **con**vict (a criminal)	con**vict** (to find guilty)
4. **ob**ject (a thing; a purpose)	ob**ject** (to be against)
5. **re**cord (a written account; a recording)	re**cord** (to write down; to make an audio- or videotape)

Exercise B

Read the following sentences aloud. Be sure to stress the first syllable of each noun and the second syllable of each verb.

1. Please **recórd** the **récord**.
2. I **objéct** to that ugly **óbject**.
3. She will **presént** you with a **présent**.
4. We **projéct** that Mario will do well on the **próject**.
5. The judge will **convíct** the **ex-cónvict**.

Exercise C

Read the following sentences aloud. Then, indicate whether the boldfaced word is a noun or a verb. Finally, circle the number of the syllable stressed.

Example

Enrique read *Reader's **Digest***.   _noun_   ① 2

1. We rode camels in the **desert**.   _____ 1   2

2. The **convict** escaped from jail.   _____ 1   2

3. They signed the **contract**.   _____ 1   2

4. Never **desert** a friend in trouble.   _____ 1   2

5. Don't **convict** me for a crime I didn't do. _____ 1   2

Chapter 7

Participating in Group Discussions

What is the difference between public speaking and group discussion? In group discussions a group of people exchange and evaluate ideas and information in order to better understand a subject or to solve a problem. It is an active and dynamic experience in which all members of the group interact and listen to each other. In contrast, the audience mainly listens to the public speaker.

When do we participate in group discussions? We participate in them all the time. In today's world, we often get together to share information, solve a common problem, or present a variety of different viewpoints to an audience. We participate in group discussions at book club, civic group, or

PTA meetings, while serving on jury duty, at lunch with friends, and during meals with our families. Group discussion is an important part of speech communication because we participate in it so often.

In this chapter, you will learn how to lead and participate in a problem-solving group discussion.

Path to Successful Problem Solving for Group Discussions

A successful group discussion is one that accomplishes objectives and improves a situation. However, many discussions are not productive because the participants wander aimlessly from point to point without any plan. In order to have a successful group discussion, it is essential to have a logical and organized plan.

Though group discussions serve a variety of purposes, the most popular purpose is to solve a problem. The following path to successful problem solving will help you organize a group discussion into a logical sequence of events so that all participants can find one or more solutions to a problem.

Path to Successful Problem Solving for Group Discussions

6. Select the Best Solutions

5. Present Possible Solutions to the Problem

4. Predict Possible Future Effects of the Problem

3. Explain the Causes of the Problem

2. Prove the Problem Exists

1. Identify a Problem

If you follow these steps, or this path, you will be able to organize your group discussion into a logical sequence of events so that all participants can find one or more solutions to a problem.

Step 1: Identify a Problem

Choose a problem that interests all participants. The discussion will be much livelier if all group members feel personally involved and committed to solving the problem.

Example
One group of students chose the problem of children in the U.S. being less physically fit than ever before.

Activity

In small groups, brainstorm (make a list of) specific problems for each category in the "Problems for Group Discussion" chart that follows.

Problems for Group Discussion

Campus Problems
Examples
auto thefts
limited access for handicapped

_____

_____

Community Problems
Examples
an unsafe intersection
unsolved hate crimes

_____

_____

City Problems
Examples
lack of housing
unreliable transit systems

_____

_____

State Problems
Examples
unemployment
insufficient funding for education

_____

_____

National Problems
Examples
drug abuse
illiteracy

_____

_____

International Problems
Examples
air pollution
human rights abuses

_____

_____

Step 2: Prove the Problem Exists

Present evidence that your group's problem truly exists. Find statistics, refer to your own personal experiences or the experiences of people you know, quote expert sources, or give specific incidences of the problem that have been reported in the news.

Example

Children in the U.S. are less physically fit than ever before.

1. The Harvard School of Public Health research has found alarming increases in the rate of obesity since 1960.

   a) Fifty-four percent increase among six- to eleven-year-olds

   b) Thirty-nine percent increase among twelve- to seventeen-year-olds

2. A Chrysler Fund Amateur Athletic Union (AAU) study found the average weight of twelve- to thirteen-year-olds has increased eight pounds over the past decade with only a slight increase in height.

3. The AAU study found that the percentage of children reaching minimal standards on four fitness tests had declined from forty-three percent to thirty-two percent.

4. The American Health Foundation reports that thirty percent of children three to eighteen years old have above-average blood cholesterol levels.

Step 3: Explain the Causes of the Problem

Present information that reveals the causes of the problem. Brainstorming can help you discover this information. As you brainstorm, follow the guidelines below:

- Think of as many ideas as you can. Anyone may contribute ideas at any time. The more ideas, the better.

- Do not criticize or evaluate ideas at this point. Even a "bad" idea may provoke a better one from someone else.

- When you can think of no more ideas, evaluate the ones your group came up with. Keep the causes that are most relevant; discard the others.

Example

Children in the U.S. are less physically fit than ever before.

1. Diets high in fat, salt, and sugar
2. Pollution and/or crime making it unsafe for children to play outside
3. TV and video games that encourage children to remain indoors
4. Deterioration of physical-fitness instruction in schools

Step 4: Predict Possible Future Effects of the Problem

Predict what is likely to happen if the problem is not solved. You could explain, for example, how people or society in general might be affected.

Example

Children in the U.S. are less physically fit than ever before.

1. There will be increased physical problems in adulthood causing much human suffering.
2. Billions of dollars will be spent on medical problems.
   a) Higher medical insurance premiums
   b) More out-of-pocket medical expenses
3. There will be lower productivity due to increased absenteeism from work.

Step 5: Present Possible Solutions to the Problem

Brainstorm ways this problem might be solved. Present suggestions made by authorities and concerned individuals. Also, give your opinions about how to solve the problem.

Example

Children in the U.S. are less physically fit than ever before.

1. Pressure local schools to offer daily physical-education classes for elementary and high school students.
2. Pressure the schools to put more emphasis on good nutrition.
3. Encourage parents to limit their children's TV and video game time.
4. Encourage parents to substitute low-fat, healthier foods for junk food.
   a) Whole-wheat crackers instead of potato chips
   b) Baked potatoes instead of french fries
5. Pressure local law enforcement officers to better patrol public playgrounds so that children and their parents are not afraid to use them.

Step 6: Select the Best Solutions

Discuss the advantages and disadvantages of each proposed solution. Select the best solutions.

Activity

1. In small groups, examine the possible solutions to the problem of children in the U.S. being less physically fit than ever before presented on page 115. What are the advantages of each solution? The disadvantages? Discuss the feasibility of the solutions for ten minutes.

2. Choose the best solutions.

3. Discuss your conclusions with the entire class.

Path to Being an Effective Group Leader

Every successful group discussion needs an effective group leader. The following path to being an effective group leader shows how to assure the success of the group discussion.

1. Introduce the Participants

Introduce the members of the group to each other and to the audience, if present.

2. State the Problem to Be Discussed

Introduce the problem to be discussed and briefly explain the organizational plan to be followed. This is similar to introducing a speech by providing a preview and an attention-getting opener, as discussed on pages 79–81 of Chapter 5: Speaking to Inform.

3. Make Sure That the Organizational Plan Is Followed

Make certain the group follows the organizational plan in order and does not skip steps. If a group member goes off on a tangent, it's your job to get him or her back on track. For example, you might say, "Let's get back to that point later," or "That's an interesting comment, but let's finish what we are currently discussing."

4. Encourage All Group Members to Participate

To encourage shy group members to speak, you might call on them by name and ask, "What do you think about that?" or "Do you have any information to add?"

5. Provide Transitions between Each Step

Summarize each step in the group discussion before going on to the next step.

> **Example**
> I'm sure you agree that we have presented some rather compelling proof that this problem exists. We will now discuss several causes of this very serious problem.

For detailed guidelines on how to use transitions, see pages 42–44 of Chapter 3: Putting Your Speech Together.

6. Bring the Discussion to a Close

After twenty to twenty-five minutes, conclude the discussion. Concluding a discussion is similar to providing a summary and memorable concluding remarks for a speech, as discussed on page 81 of Chapter 5: Speaking to Inform.

7. Thank the Participants

After concluding the discussion, be sure to thank the participants for their time and hard work. If an audience is present, thank them for listening.

Path to Being a Responsible Group Member

In addition to having an effective group leader, every group discussion needs responsible and enthusiastic participants who are committed to the discussion's success. Each participant should prepare by reading and thinking about the topic beforehand. During the discussion, participants should feel free to comment, ask questions, and share information. All participants must be prepared and alert during the entire discussion. The following path to being a responsible group member below will help assure an animated and productive group discussion.

1. Be Prepared with Evidence

Prepare for the discussion by researching quotations, facts, statistics, and examples. Write possible contributions for each step of the discussion on note cards so that you can refer to them as needed during the discussion.

2. Make a Sufficient Number of Contributions

Try to contribute once or twice during each step of the discussion. This means that the group should hear from each member at least six times. Your comments don't need to be lengthy. Talk when you have a thought to share, a question to ask, or when you feel a point needs to be clarified for the audience.

3. Don't Monopolize the Discussion

Don't interrupt other group members while they are speaking. Give all participants a chance to speak and express themselves.

4. Be Open-Minded

Acknowledge other peoples' opinions and their right to express them. If you disagree with someone's opinion, let the person express the idea completely without interrupting. If you want to introduce a contrary point of view, do so politely. For example, you could start by saying "I see your point. However, …"

5. Pay Close Attention to Other Participants' Contributions

Listen carefully to other participants' ideas. Taking notes will help you to remember what they have said. You may be asked to help the group leader summarize each step in the discussion.

6. Refer to All Participants by Name

Whether you refer to them directly or indirectly, use participants' names. For example, don't point to Marisela and say, "I'd like to add to what *she* said." Say, "I'd like to add to what *Marisela* said."

Assignment

Have a group discussion on a topic of your choice.

1. In small groups, choose a leader.

2. Choose a specific problem that interests all group members and can be researched easily.

3. On your own, research the problem.

4. Complete as much of the Group Discussion Worksheet on pages 120–121 as possible. If you are the group leader, also complete the Group Leader Worksheet on page 122.

5. Your teacher may use the forms on pages 192–194 to evaluate individual members, the group leader, and the group as a whole. Look the forms over so you know exactly how you will be evaluated.

6. Using the steps on pages 113–115, discuss the problem for twenty to twenty-five minutes. Write any additional information on the Group Discussion Worksheet.

Group Discussion Worksheet

1. Identify a problem that interests all group members.

_____

2. Summarize proof that the problem exists.

_____

_____

_____

_____

3. Explain the causes of the problem.

_____

_____

_____

_____

4. Predict possible future effects of the problem.

_____

_____

_____

_____

(Continued)

5. Present possible solutions to the problem.

_____

_____

_____

_____

6. Determine the advantages and disadvantages of each solution.

Solution A: _____

Advantages: _____

Disadvantages: _____

Solution B: _____

Advantages: _____

Disadvantages: _____

Solution C: _____

Advantages: _____

Disadvantages: _____

Solution D: _____

Advantages: _____

Disadvantages: _____

7. Select the best solutions.

_____

_____

_____

Group Leader Worksheet

1. Prepare the introduction. (Introduce the participants.)

_____

_____

2. Prepare the preview. (State the problem to be discussed and the organizational plan to be followed.)

_____

_____

3. Prepare the first transition (between "Identify a Problem" and "Prove the Problem Exists").

_____

_____

4. Prepare the second transition (between "Prove the Problem Exists" and "Explain the Causes of the Problem").

_____

_____

5. Prepare the third transition (between "Explain the Causes of the Problem" and "Predict Possible Future Effects of the Problem").

_____

_____

6. Prepare the fourth transition (between "Predict Possible Future Effects of the Problem" and "Present Possible Solutions to the Problem").

_____

_____

7. Prepare the fifth transition (between "Present Possible Solutions to the Problem" and "Select the Best Solution").

_____

_____

8. Prepare memorable concluding remarks.

_____

_____

Pronunciation Tip

SENTENCE STRESS

Just as it's awkward to give all syllables in a word equal or incorrect stress, it's unnatural to stress all the words in a sentence in the same way. Effective use of strong and weak stress in phrases and sentences will help you sound like a native English speaker.

Content words (e.g., nouns, verbs, adjectives, adverbs, and question words), or words that convey meaning, are the important words in a sentence. We usually stress them when speaking. On the other hand, function words (e.g., articles and prepositions) don't carry as much meaning as content words and are less important. We usually do not stress them when speaking.

 Exercise A

Read the following expressions aloud. Be sure to stress the content words, not the function words.

1. in a **moment**
2. to **tell** the **truth**
3. **Silence** is **golden**.
4. **Honesty** is the **best policy**.
5. A **penny saved** is a **penny earned**.

6. as **good** as **gold**
7. as **light** as a **feather**
8. It's **now** or **never**.
9. **luck** of the **draw**
10. as **dry** as a **bone**

Speakers sometimes stress certain words in a sentence to call attention to them. This can change the meaning, or focus, of the sentence.

Example

He is my speech teacher. (This emphasizes *who* the teacher is.)
He is *my* speech teacher. (This emphasizes that it is the *speaker's* teacher.)
He is my **speech** teacher. (This emphasizes *what kind of* teacher he is.)

 Exercise B

Read the following sentences aloud. Be sure to stress the boldfaced words.

1. Mary is Anne's **friend**. She **isn't** her cousin.
2. John is **married** to Anne. They **aren't** engaged.
3. They **own** a small home. They don't **rent**.
4. They live in Washington, **D.C.**, **not** Washington State.
5. Anne will open a **pet** store, **not** a toy store.

Exercise C

Practice reading the following dialog aloud with a classmate. Be sure to stress the boldfaced words.

JOHN: Anne, who was on the **phone**?

ANNE: My old friend, **Mary**.

JOHN: Mary **Jones**?

ANNE: No, Mary **Hall**.

JOHN: I don't know Mary **Hall**. Where is she **from**?

ANNE: She's from **Washington**.

JOHN: Washington, the **state**, or Washington, the **city**?

ANNE: Washington, **D.C.**, our nation's **capital**.

JOHN: Is that where she **lives**?

ANNE: Yes, she still lives in the white **house**.

JOHN: The **White** House? With the **president**?

ANNE: No, silly. The white **house** on **First** Street.

JOHN: What did she **want**?

ANNE: She wants to **come** here.

JOHN: Come **here**? **When**?

ANNE: In a **week**. She's bringing her black **bird**, her **collie**, her **snakes**, her …

JOHN: **Stop**! She's bringing a **zoo** to our house?

ANNE: No, John. She's opening a **pet** store here in **town**.

Chapter 8

Understanding Interpersonal Communication

Interpersonal communication is all around us. It occurs anytime people exchange messages—when they express their opinions, ask and answer questions, express how they feel, talk about what they like and dislike, or say what they want and don't want.

When do we communicate interpersonally? We do it all the time. Whenever we talk to friends, parents, children, teachers, employers, waiters, doctors, sales clerks—in short, anyone—we are communicating interpersonally. Sometimes our communication is successful and we feel very good about it. However, sometimes it is not so successful. We may have an unpleasant argument or misunderstanding that causes us to feel angry, confused, or upset.

In this chapter, you will learn how to avoid misunderstandings in interpersonal communication. You will learn techniques of effective interpersonal communication that will help you feel good about yourself and your interactions with others.

Warm Up

Find out more about how your classmates perceive themselves and each other.

1. In small groups, choose a group leader.

2. On a blank sheet of paper, write:

    I think that most people in this group see me as _____, _____, and _____. However, I really am _____, _____, and _____.

    Fill in the blanks with adjectives or descriptive phrases. Do not let anyone see your responses and do not write your name on the paper.

3. Give your paper to the group leader.

4. The leader reads each statement. Try to guess who wrote each statement. Explain your reasons.

5. When everyone has finished guessing, identify which statement you wrote.

6. As a class, discuss whether you were surprised by what any of the group members wrote. If so, which ones? Why? Do you think people perceive you differently from how you perceive yourself? If so, why?

Avoiding Miscommunications

Misunderstandings happen to everyone. They occur between friends, coworkers, lovers, and family members. Communication breakdowns can be as harmless as showing up for an appointment a half hour early or as inconvenient as waiting in the rain for two hours for someone who never shows up. They can be as devastating as a broken relationship or a divorce. They can even be a matter of life and death. For example, failure to communicate fuel shortages and other mechanical problems has been the cause of some airline disasters.

Miscommunication often occurs because listeners assume they understand what a speaker means, when, in fact, the speaker had intended a completely different meaning from what was understood.

Example: Susana's Story

Susana was generally too shy to speak up in class. She finally had the courage to ask her psychology professor a question during a lecture. Before answering her, he replied, "Now that's an unusual query." Susana felt insulted, as she believed that her professor was implying that her question was foolish. She told the story to her speech communication professor in tears. Her speech communication professor was sure that the psychology professor hadn't intended to belittle Susana and encouraged her to ask him what he had really meant. The psychology professor was upset that Susana had misinterpreted his comment, as he had intended it to be a compliment. He had meant that her question was intelligent and insightful.

Sometimes, when listeners misunderstand what was said, they blame the speaker as being the source of the problem or misunderstanding without taking the time to ask the speaker for clarification. Other listeners simply ignore messages they don't understand or say the messages don't make any sense.

Much miscommunication can be avoided by determining what certain words mean before criticizing the speaker or the message. It's important to say to oneself, "I don't understand the message. I had better ask some questions about it. It might mean something else to another person."

Activity

Compare your understanding of a message with what the author intended.

1. Read the following information about Donna:

   Donna was levelheaded and giddy. She was kind and silly. Donna was tiny but so large that everyone admired her.

2. What is your first impression of the above information? Write it below.

   _____

   _____

3. Be prepared to discuss your impression in class. Did you think the words were contradictory or nonsensical?

Think about this: With today's meaning of some words, this message does indeed sound like nonsense. However, in early English, many of the words used had completely different definitions from what they mean today. *Giddy* used to mean "enthusiastic" or "divinely possessed," derived from the same root as *God*. *Silly* once meant "happy," coming from the German word *soelig*. *Large* meant "good-hearted" or "generous." If you substitute these definitions, the paragraph means:

Donna was levelheaded and enthusiastic. She was kind and happy. Donna was tiny but so generous that everyone admired her.

Now that the words seem to make more sense, you are less likely to reject them, call them nonsense, or criticize the author. If people made a consistent effort to look beyond a speaker's actual words to find out what they mean, misunderstandings would occur much less frequently.

Clarifying the Speaker's Intentions

Sometimes listeners jump to conclusions and blame their misunderstandings on the speaker without first clarifying his or her intentions. For instance, Susana jumped to the hasty conclusion that *unusual* meant "foolish" and that her professor was insulting her. Clarifying a speaker's message can help avoid misunderstandings and subsequent bad feelings.

Example: Peggy and Anne's Story

Peggy was expecting a delivery and knew she would not be home to accept it. She requested that the delivery service leave the parcel with her neighbor Anne. Happy to help, Anne brought the small package to Peggy's home after dinner. Peggy exclaimed, "I'm sure glad you didn't know what was in the box. Those are the diamond earrings my daughter sent for my birthday."

Anne's first reaction was to feel slighted. She assumed that Peggy was implying that she was dishonest and that she would have stolen the package if she had known it was valuable. However, Anne realized she might have misinterpreted Peggy's remarks so, she asked, "Why are you glad I didn't know what was in the box?" Peggy replied, "Because had you known, you might have been unwilling to be responsible for such a valuable package." Anne was extremely relieved to learn that Peggy hadn't meant that she was untrustworthy. Had Anne not made the effort to clear up the misunderstanding, she would have harbored feelings of ill will toward Peggy. Their friendship would have deteriorated without Peggy ever knowing why.

Anne effectively avoided a miscommunication by asking Peggy to clarify what she had meant. If you are upset or confused about somebody's message, ask yourself, "Could I be misinterpreting what was said?" Getting the answer is as simple as asking, "I'm not sure what you meant. Would you please explain?"

Activity

Describe a personal experience in which a miscommunication occurred.

1. Think of a miscommunication you have had. Prepare answers to the following questions:

   a) Why did the miscommunication occur?

   b) How might the miscommunication have been avoided?

   c) Was the misunderstanding resolved? If so, how? If not, what could be done now to resolve it?

2. In small groups, describe the miscommunication. Be sure to answer the questions above. Be prepared to answer any other questions from the group.

Interpersonal Communication Styles

There are three possible broad approaches to the conduct of interpersonal relations. The first is to consider one's self only and ride roughshod over others. The second is always to put others before one's self. The third approach is the golden mean. The individual places himself first but takes others into account.

— Joseph Wolpe, M.D., *The Practice of Behavior Therapy*

The first interpersonal communication approach Dr. Wolpe describes is called the *aggressive* style. The second is called the *submissive* style. The third approach, the *golden mean*, is the one Dr. Wolpe recommends above all the others. It is referred to as the *assertive* style.

People who use the aggressive style of communication appear to be somewhat belligerent. They deliver their messages in loud, hostile voices which convey the impression that they believe their opinions and feelings are more important than anyone else's. Intentionally or unintentionally, aggressive communicators tend to embarrass, insult, or intimidate their listeners in order to get their way.

People who use the submissive style of communication appear to put themselves last and seem to consider themselves inferior to others. This style encourages others to disregard their needs and to take advantage of them. Intentionally or unintentionally, submissive communicators often don't get what they want because they don't stand up for themselves.

People who use the assertive communication style appear to have a healthy self-image. They express their wishes in a clear and direct way that conveys the impression that they expect their rights to be respected and that they, in turn, respect the rights of others. Assertive speakers appear to be positive, fair, and self-confident.

The following chart illustrates the key characteristics of the three interpersonal communication styles.

Style	Characteristic
aggressive	I'm important. You're not important.
submissive	I'm not important. You're important.
assertive	We're both important.

The following examples illustrate how people with submissive, aggressive, and assertive styles of interpersonal communication might respond to different situations.

Example A: A smoker asks if you object to his or her smoking in your car. You are allergic to smoke.

Aggressive Response: Yes, I most certainly do object. You are very rude and inconsiderate to even consider subjecting me to secondhand smoke. I refuse to allow smoking in my car.

Submissive Response: No problem, that's fine if you really want to.

Assertive Response: Thank you for asking. I'd prefer you didn't. It really bothers me. Would you like me to pull over so you could smoke a cigarette outside? I'd be happy to stop whenever you like.

Example B: You're next in line at a checkout counter and are in a hurry to leave. Somebody says, "Excuse me, I'm late for an important meeting. May I go ahead of you?"

Aggressive Response: Absolutely not! Go to the end of the line like everybody else!

Submissive Response: Sure, OK.

Assertive Response: Actually, I'm also in a hurry. Why don't you ask someone in a different line?

Being aware of these three interpersonal communication styles will help you recognize your usual style and that of the people you know. With practice, you can become more skillful at using an assertive style, the *golden mean*, in your interactions with others.

Exercise

For each response to the following situations, circle the letter of the communication style used:

A   aggressive   B   submissive   C   assertive

1. You are in a restaurant and order your meal with a plain baked potato. It is served to you with butter and sour cream.

   a) You reprimand the server for not paying better attention to your order and for not checking the food before serving it.   A   B   C

   b) You remind the server that you had requested a plain potato and ask him or her to bring you another one.   A   B   C

   c) You either eat the potato as is or leave it uneaten on your plate without mentioning the error.   A   B   C

2. While waiting in line to buy movie tickets, someone cuts in front of you.

   a) You say nothing, hoping someone behind you will complain.   A   B   C

   b) You admonish the person for being rude and loudly tell him or her to wait like everyone else.   A   B   C

   c) You say that you had arrived first and point out the end of the line in case the person hadn't realized his or her mistake.   A   B   C

3. Your teacher returns your exam after grading it. He or she marked an answer wrong that you're sure is correct.

   a) You wait until after class and then show your teacher the exam. You explain that you don't understand why your answer was marked wrong and ask if it could be an oversight on his or her part.   A   B   C

   b) When you notice the error, you interrupt the lecture. Waving your exam in the air, you say, "You made a mistake grading my paper. I want you to correct it right now."   A   B   C

   c) You rationalize that the question was only worth three points and decide not to bring the error to your teacher's attention.   A   B   C

Activity

Read the following situations. Think of assertive, submissive, and aggressive responses to each one. Write them in the spaces provided.

1. After waiting for your car to be serviced at the dealership, the service manager tells you it's ready. You go outside prepared to drive away. The car hasn't been washed, and the mechanics have left the windows and floor mats filthy. Handing you the keys, the service manager thanks you for your business.

   a) aggressive response: _____

   _____

   b) submissive response: _____

   _____

   c) assertive response: _____

   _____

2. A delivery person brings you a pizza loaded with anchovies, mushrooms, and sausage. You specifically ordered one with double cheese only.

   a) aggressive response: _____

   _____

   b) submissive response: _____

   _____

   c) assertive response: _____

   _____

3. You and a friend are seated in a crowded movie theater. All the seats are taken. The loud conversation of the couple sitting next to you is distracting.

   a) aggressive response: _____

   _____

   b) submissive response: _____

   _____

c) assertive response: _____

_____

4. Your roommates are pressuring you to move with them into a more expensive apartment. You really can't afford to pay more rent; besides, you like your current apartment. You're worried that they'll resent you if you don't agree to their request.

a) aggressive response: _____

_____

b) submissive response: _____

_____

c) assertive response: _____

_____

Direct and Indirect Communication Styles

Many individuals are reluctant to state their feelings clearly and directly. They may have a tendency to hint at what they want, or "beat around the bush," by phrasing their needs and wants as questions rather than statements. This manner of communication can be very confusing and frustrating to listeners.

In an article for the *Washington Post*, Deborah Tannen, Ph.D., presents an illustration of how some people communicate indirectly by expressing their wishes as questions. A couple was having a conversation while riding in their car. The wife asked, "Would you like to stop for a drink?" Her husband answered "No," and they didn't stop. He was later frustrated to learn that his wife was annoyed because she had wanted to stop for a drink. He wondered, "Why didn't she just say what she wanted? Why did she play games with me?"

Phrasing your requests as questions can lead to confusion and misunderstanding. People will take your needs and wants much more seriously if you express them using a direct and assertive interpersonal communication style.

Activity A

Read each situation. Replace each question with a direct statement.

Example

Your younger brother is playing his stereo so loud that you can't concentrate on your studying. You go into his room and ask, "Don't you think the music is a bit loud?" You really mean,

Please lower the volume. I'm studying for an exam.

1. You and a friend have gone out to dinner in a restaurant. You don't like the location of the table where the host or hostess is taking you. You ask, "Isn't this table stuck away in the corner?" You really mean,

   _____

   _____

2. You and your date have been at a party for hours. You feel very tired and want to go home desperately. You turn to your date and ask, "Are you ready to leave yet?" You really mean,

   _____

   _____

3. You're at a friend's house on a chilly winter day. Several windows are open and you are freezing. You ask your friend, "Isn't it a bit cold in here?" You really mean,

   _____

   _____

4. You're at the library trying to study. Several other students are carrying on a loud conversation that you find distracting. You go over to them and ask them, "Isn't there some place else you guys can go to have a conversation?" You really mean,

   _____

   _____

5. A passenger in your car lights a cigarette. You really don't like people to smoke in your car. You ask, "Do you have to smoke that in here?" You really mean,

   _____

   _____

Activity B

1. Think of ten situations in which you are reluctant to speak up or take action. Use the following situations or situations of your own:

   - Speaking up about receiving a lesser product or service than you expected
   - Sending back improperly prepared food in a restaurant
   - Calling attention to an overcharge in a bill
   - Declining an invitation to a social event or for a date
   - Saying "no" to unwanted houseguests
   - Asking a friend to return money that he or she borrowed
   - Speaking up if someone cuts in front of you in line
   - Returning a defective product to a store
   - Speaking up to a colleague who calls you by a nickname you don't like
   - Saying "no" to a friend's request to borrow a favorite possession

2. Rank the situations from 1 to 10, 1 being the situation in which it is most difficult for you to assert yourself. Write them in the chart that follows.

Rank	Situation
1	
2	
3	
4	
5	
6	
7	
8	
9	
10	

3. In small groups, discuss the situations you wrote down and how you would like to respond to each one.

Assignment

Role-play assertive interpersonal communication.

1. Choose a situation from Activity B on page 135.

2. With a partner, discuss what you'd like to do and say in that situation.

3. Role-play the situation with your partner. Practice responding assertively.

4. Present the role-play to the class.

Pronunciation Tip

[s], [t], AND [θ]

A common error is to pronounce the sound [s] or [t] instead of the sound [θ] (as in *thin*). If you substitute [s] for [θ], **thank** will sound like **sank**. If you substitute [t] for [θ], **three** will sound like **tree**.

Pronounce [θ] by placing your tongue between your teeth. Pronounce [s] and [t] by placing your tongue behind your teeth. Look in a mirror and make sure you can see the tip of your tongue when you pronounce [θ]. Make sure you cannot see it when you pronounce [s] and [t].

 ### Exercise A

Read the following words aloud. Look in a mirror and make sure you can see and feel the tip of your tongue between your teeth.

1. **th**ing
2. **th**ink
3. **th**ought
4. **th**rough
5. **Th**ursday
6. heal**th**y
7. weal**th**y
8. some**th**ing

9. ba**th**tub
10. bir**th**day
11. too**th**
12. bo**th**
13. ear**th**
14. fai**th**
15. brea**th**

Exercise B

Read the following sets of words aloud. Be sure to place your tongue between your teeth when pronouncing [θ] and behind your teeth when pronouncing [s] and [t].

[θ]	[s]	[t]
1. **th**ree	**s**ee	**t**ea
2. **th**in	**s**in	**t**in
3. **th**igh	**s**igh	**t**ie
4. ba**th**	ba**ss**	ba**t**
5. fai**th**	fa**ce**	fa**te**

 Exercise C

Read the following phrases and sentences aloud. Be sure to place your tongue between your teeth when pronouncing [θ].

1. a) **thirty-third**

   b) **Thelma** had her **thirty-third birthday**.

2. a) **Thanksgiving**

   b) **Thanksgiving** falls on **Thursday**.

3. a) **through thick** and **thin**

   b) We remained friends **through thick** and **thin**.

4. a) **something** for **nothing**

   b) Don't **think** you can get **something** for **nothing**.

5. a) **author's theme**

   b) The **author's theme** is **thought**-provoking.

Chapter 9

Understanding Intercultural Communication

According to the chapter on gestures, they're either waving hello or warning us of danger.

What is *intercultural communication*? In order to understand what this term means, it is important to first understand the term *culture*. Culture involves the beliefs, values, and behavioral patterns shared by large groups of people. It is learned from one's parents, family, friends, and other people one interacts with throughout one's life. No culture is better than another; it is simply different.

Intercultural communication occurs when people from different cultures exchange information, ideas, thoughts, and feelings with one another. They may do this through speaking, writing, or gestures. Sometimes, due to different beliefs, values, or behavioral patterns, miscommunication occurs. In order to communicate effectively across cultures, it is important to understand, respect, and appreciate the diverse beliefs and customs of people from different cultures.

The exercises and activities in this chapter are designed to help you gain an awareness and appreciation for cultural differences so that you can communicate across cultures more effectively.

Warm Up

Find out more about beliefs, values, and behavioral patterns in different cultures.

1. In your culture, what is true about the people below? Write statements.

Examples

Men *are usually responsible for earning money.*

Women *are usually in charge of family finances.*

Young children *rarely help with the housework.*

a) Men _____

b) Women _____

c) Young children _____

d) Fathers _____

e) Mothers _____

f) Husbands _____

g) Wives _____

h) Brothers _____

i) Sisters _____

j) Grandparents _____

k) Single men _____

l) Single women _____

m) Teachers _____

n) Students _____

o) Neighbors _____

2. In small groups, compare your statements. Discuss the following questions.

   a) Which of your statements were similar?

   b) Which of your statements were different?

   c) Which of your statements surprised you?

Ethnocentricity

Ethnocentricity refers to the attitude that one's culture is better than any other culture. People who demonstrate cultural ethnocentricity look down on other cultures and believe them to be deficient in some way.

People can be ethnocentric about their country, looking down on people from other countries. They can be ethnocentric about religion or politics, believing themselves to be superior to those who have different views. They can even be ethnocentric about geography. For example, some city dwellers feel superior to those who live in rural areas, believing them to be less sophisticated and less educated.

Example: Belinda's Story

An American student, Belinda, described how she and her family moved from New York City to Montana. Belinda's friends felt sorry for her because she was leaving Fifth Avenue and Broadway behind. Belinda was unhappy because she thought she was moving to a primitive place. At first, her ethnocentric attitude prevented her from appreciating what Montana had to offer. Fortunately, after some initial adjustment, Belinda learned to love the beauty of the state, the friendliness of the people, and the other benefits of living in Montana.

Stereotypes

A *stereotype* refers to a preconceived idea about a person's gender, profession, race, religion, or culture. For example, statements like "All women love to shop," "All men like sports," "All accountants are boring," and "All New Yorkers are rude" are based on stereotypes. If you look closely at most stereotypes, you'll find that they are inaccurate and oversimplified. People from the same background all differ, and no two members of any culture behave alike all the time.

Activity A

Find out more about stereotypes in general.

1. Complete each statement with an adjective that describes your culture's reactions to these animals.

   a) All snakes are _____

   b) All lions are _____

   c) All fish are _____

   d) All dogs are _____

   e) All cats are _____

   f) All pigs are _____

   g) All spiders are _____

   h) All birds are _____

   i) All rats are _____

   j) All horses are _____

2. In small groups, compare your answers. Discuss the following questions:

   a) Did you have difficulty completing each sentence with just one word? If so, why?

   b) Did everyone agree on the same adjective for any of the statements? If so, which one(s)?

   c) Were any animals given many different adjectives? If so, which one(s)?

In the exercise above, it may have been hard to fill in each blank with just one word because it is difficult to stereotype animals. Some snakes are poisonous; some are harmless. There are many breeds of dogs, including poodles, Doberman pinschers, cocker spaniels, and sheepdogs, each of which is often given a stereotype. Some are presumed to be sweet and lovable while others are reputed to be vicious and mean. It's unreasonable to describe *all* snakes, *all* spiders, or *all* dogs with one adjective, yet *all* members of one culture are often ascribed the same quality. Unfortunately, this quality is often a negative one.

Activity B

Discuss how cultural stereotypes affect intercultural communication.

1. Explain a stereotype that others have of people from your culture.
2. Do you think this stereotype is accurate? Why or why not?
3. What reasons can you give for this stereotype?
4. How do you feel about this stereotype? Why?
5. Does this stereotype ever interfere with effective intercultural communication? If so, how?

Activity C

Stereotypes often occur when people misinterpret cultural differences. How would you interpret the attitude of students who behave in the following manners? Write your answers in the spaces provided. Then compare your answers in small groups.

Student's Behavior	Interpretation
sits at the back of the classroom and does not participate in class discussions	
acts extremely embarrassed when called on by the teacher	
constantly apologizes	
asks lots of questions	
offers opinions frequently without being asked	
never offers opinions, even when asked	
doesn't look at other people when speaking	
shrugs shoulders when asked questions	
says "yes" to everything	

Cultural Differences in Communication

Intercultural communication is really interpersonal communication between people from different cultures. Although individuals within a culture differ, similarities in communication styles exist within each culture. In some cultures, people are generally very direct. They value free speech and express their personal opinions openly and assertively, saying exactly what they mean. People from such countries as Israel, the United States, Canada, Australia, New Zealand, and Great Britain tend to communicate rather directly relative to people from other countries. On the other hand, people from such countries as Japan, China, Korea, Thailand, and Mexico tend to communicate relatively indirectly. In order to maintain harmony and avoid conflict, they rarely express disagreement or displeasure in public for fear they might offend someone. They value silence and tend to speak in roundabout ways that individuals from cultures with more direct communication styles find confusing.

If, for example, a person bought an item that turned out to be defective, his or her response to the situation would likely be influenced by his or her culture. A person from a culture with a direct communication style would likely show it to a customer service representative. He or she might say, "Excuse me, this product is defective. I would like a refund, please." If refused, the person might ask to see the manager and repeat the request. On the other hand, a person from a culture with a more indirect communication style might not even return the product to the store. If he or she did, that person might show it to a customer service representative, apologize for being a bother, and hope that the representative would take the initiative to offer a refund. Alternatively, that person might display the defective item and ask, "Is there something you can do about this?" in the hope of being offered a refund without directly requesting one. If that person's request were denied, he or she would probably thank the employee and leave the store without pursuing the matter further.

Nonverbal Communication

Nonverbal communication, such as posture, facial expressions, eye contact, body movements, and gestures, also differs between cultures. These differences are discussed in detail in Chapter 2: Delivering Your Message. A lack of awareness about these differences can lead to frustration, annoyance, and misunderstandings.

Example: Ruth Ann's Story

   Ruth Ann was an American student in a freshman science class. Her teacher assigned her to work on a project with a partner. Her partner, an exchange student, was from a culture in which direct eye contact is considered rude and disrespectful. Whenever Ruth Ann tried to engage him in conversation, he looked down at the floor. She thought that her partner was not interested in what she had to say and became very frustrated. Finally, during a work session, she placed both of her hands on his shoulders and said loudly, "Look at me when I'm speaking to you." This made her partner feel extremely self-conscious and uncomfortable.

   Ruth Ann didn't realize that her classmate hadn't meant to slight her; he was simply displaying nonverbal behavior characteristic of his own culture. If she had been more aware of this, she probably wouldn't have gotten frustrated and made him uncomfortable.

Activity

Read the following story. As a class, discuss the questions that follow.

Example: Tomiko's Story

   Tomiko was a Japanese student enrolled in Professor Johnson's class. One day, Professor Johnson was coming out of a classroom after giving a workshop on listening. Tomiko timidly approached her without saying a word. Professor Johnson, in an effort to engage Tomiko in conversation, asked her, "Did you enjoy the workshop?" "Yes, yes, I very much enjoyed the workshop," replied Tomiko, who then continued to talk about how much she had gained from the workshop. Professor Johnson, carrying a full load of books and papers to grade, politely listened and thanked Tomiko for her compliments, but Tomiko continued to stand in front of her.

   Professor Johnson was confused. She didn't want to seem rude, but she was frustrated and impatient because she had a lot of work to do, and Tomiko wasn't asking any specific questions. Finally, Professor Johnson asked Tomiko if she would like a schedule of upcoming workshops to be offered. "Yes," replied Tomiko shyly with her head bowed, "I would like that very much."

1. How did Tomiko feel about her interaction with Professor Jones?
2. How did her cultural background influence her communication style?
3. How did Professor Jones feel about her interaction with Tomiko?
4. How did her cultural background influence her communication style?

5. What could Tomiko have done to communicate more effectively?

6. What could Professor Jones have done to communicate more effectively?

Can you think of any situations in which you might have misunderstood someone's behavior because of his or her cultural background? If so, how could the misunderstanding have been avoided? How can similar misunderstandings be avoided in the future? What factors should be considered when trying to establish communication with a person from another culture?

Assignment

Role-play different communication styles and discuss how they differ across cultures.

1. With a partner, choose one of the following situations:
   - You are a university student. You want to get to know an attractive student in your class. You would like the student to join you for a cup of coffee after class.
   - You are a loyal, hardworking employee. You have been working for the same company for two years and have not received a raise. You would like your boss to give you a raise.
   - You are a student. Your classmate borrowed a book from you and hasn't returned it. You need the book to study for an exam. You would like your classmate to return the book.
   - You are a newlywed. You are shopping for furniture with your spouse. Your spouse likes furniture that you think is ugly. You would like to buy different furniture.
   - You are a student. Your teacher has made a mistake in calculating your grade on an exam so that you received 83 percent instead of 89 percent. You would like the mistake corrected.

2. Prepare two skits about the situation you have chosen. In the first skit, role-play the situation using an *indirect* communication style. For example, hint at what you want or express your wishes as questions. In the second skit, role-play the situation using a *direct* communication style. For example, state your wishes explicitly.

3. Role-play the two skits in front of the class.

4. As a class, discuss the two skits. Which style are you more comfortable with? Which style is closer to that used in your culture? How would the situation be handled differently in your culture?

Assignment

Explain or speculate how a belief, value, or behavioral pattern from your culture is perceived by people from other cultures.

1. Think of a custom, common practice, or behavior that is characteristic of your culture or the culture of someone you know well.

2. Explain the custom or practice.

3. Describe how a person from another culture reacted or might react to the custom or practice.

Example A: Opening Christmas Presents

My friend Mary's family doesn't open their Christmas presents on Christmas Day. They get together on Christmas Eve to exchange gifts. Mary's great-grandfather came from Norway. It is a Norwegian custom to open presents on Christmas Eve. This became the tradition in Mary's family. Mary's new husband, John, was surprised and shocked by this custom. His family had always opened presents on Christmas Day. Mary and John decided to compromise and open half of their presents on Christmas Eve and the other half of their presents on Christmas Day.

Example B: Making Tea

Ish, a student at the University of Florida, had just arrived from rural India. He ordered a cup of tea in the student cafeteria. He had never used or seen a tea bag. An American classmate, Josh, watched in amazement as Ish tore open the tea bag and emptied its contents into his cup of hot water. Josh got Ish another cup of hot water and a new tea bag, and showed Ish how to dip the tea bag in the water. Ish then proceeded to immerse a paper packet of sugar in the hot water as well. Josh got his new friend yet another cup of hot water, and explained that we tear open sugar packets first and discard the paper wrapper. Poor Ish was extremely confused!

Thanks to all the technological advances that have connected people from different countries, the world is becoming a smaller place. In the future, you will be communicating more and more with people from different backgrounds. Appreciating and valuing cultural differences helps to promote human understanding and successful interaction among people from diverse cultures. Practicing effective intercultural communication will prepare you for informed and compassionate involvement in our increasingly global society.

CONTRACTIONS

A contraction is the short form of a word or words. For example, the contraction of **do not** is **don't**, and the contraction of **did not** is **didn't**. Contractions are frequently used in spoken English and are grammatically correct.

When participating in conversations, use contractions. They will make your speech sound smooth and natural.

Exercise A

Write the contraction of each two-word expression. Read each expression and its contraction aloud.

Example: it is ___it's___

1. does not _____
2. I am _____
3. should not _____
4. will not _____
5. he is _____

6. I will _____
7. cannot _____
8. we have _____
9. you are _____
10. is not _____

Exercise B

Write ten sentences using contractions from Exercise A. Read them aloud.

1. _____
2. _____
3. _____
4. _____
5. _____
6. _____
7. _____
8. _____
9. _____
10. _____

Exercise C

Read the following pairs of sentences aloud. Notice how smooth, natural, and informal the sentences with contractions sound compared to those using the uncontracted forms.

1. a) Omar **does not** know.

   b) Omar **doesn't** know.

2. a) I **do not** think she cares.

   b) I **don't** think she cares.

3. a) **You are** coming, **are you not**?

   b) **You're** coming, **aren't you**?

4. a) **She is** very tall.

   b) **She's** very tall.

5. a) Antonio **is not** a good cook.

   b) Antonio **isn't** a good cook.

Chapter 10

Thinking on Your Feet

Thinking is something people do all day long. "Thinking on your feet" means being able to organize one's ideas quickly and speak about a subject without advance time to prepare. This type of speech is often called an *impromptu speech*.

When do we make impromptu speeches? We make them all the time. Most of our conversations with friends, parents, teachers, and employers are really short impromptu talks. These impromptu talks might include answering questions, giving opinions, or sharing knowledge about the many topics we discuss with people on a daily basis. As you can see, you already have experience giving impromptu speeches.

In this chapter, you will learn how to think on your feet and give short speeches without advance preparation.

Warm Up

One way to improve your ability to give impromptu speeches is to practice giving extended responses to questions. The following activities will develop your capability to think on your feet, organize your ideas quickly, and speak informatively and confidently about a variety of topics.

Activity A

Practice giving a short impromptu speech in response to an open-ended (information or *Wh-*) question. Explain your opinion by giving examples and reasons.

1. Your teacher will ask you an open-ended (information or *Wh-*) question. Possible questions include:
   - Who is the best teacher you've ever had?
   - What do you look for in a friend?
   - What is your favorite city?
   - What is your favorite holiday?
   - Why do people get married?
   - What do you like best about living in this country?
   - How are teachers in your country different from those in this country?
   - How do you feel about divorce?
   - What is your favorite time of year?
   - How do you feel about capital punishment?

2. Think about the question for a minute. Consider examples and reasons that will support your answer.

3. Give a one to two minute speech in which you answer the question.

Activity B

Practice giving a short impromptu response to a closed-ended (yes/no) question. Elaborate on your thoughts by anticipating what the listener might want to know and providing that information.

Example

Question: Do you go to school?

Answer A: Yes. (*This is a superficial response.*)

Answer B: Yes, I'm a junior at Northeastern University, and I'm majoring in business administration. I like the facilities at the university a lot, especially the sports facilities. The program is challenging, but the professors are very helpful. (*This is an elaborate response.*)

1. Your teacher will ask you a closed-ended question. Possible questions include:

   - Do you go to school?
   - Do you like animals?
   - Do you live near here?
   - Did you study English before coming here?
   - Do you have any pets?
   - Are you a good cook?
   - Do you have any siblings?
   - Do you like to watch TV?
   - Would you like to have children one day?
   - Do you believe in extrasensory perception?

2. Think about the question for a minute. What follow-up information could you provide to make your response more interesting?

3. Answer the question as completely as possible.

Preparing for the Impromptu Speech

The best preparation for an impromptu speech is to be well-informed about people, places, and news events in your city, state, country, and around the world. This type of information will enable you to speak informatively about many topics in different situations.

Assignment

The following assignments will help you become better informed. This will make you better able to speak about many topics when asked to make impromptu speeches. Choose one and be prepared to talk about it in class.

1. Watch the evening news on TV. Be prepared to describe the details of a news story.

2. Listen to a radio news station for ten minutes. Choose a news item that interests you. Be prepared to describe it and explain why you found it interesting.

3. Read the editorial page of your local newspaper. Be prepared to give an oral summary of an editorial about a controversial issue and explain why you agree or disagree with the editor's opinions.

4. Choose an article from a national newsmagazine like *Time*, *Newsweek*, or *U.S. News and World Report* that you feel is very important. Be prepared to talk about the article and explain why it is important.

5. Describe a news event to three different people outside of class. Ask them their opinions about what you read or heard. Be prepared to discuss their opinions about the news event.

Organizing the Impromptu Speech

In preparing for an impromptu speech, it is important to become familiar with different organizational patterns. Familiarization with such patterns will enable you to choose the best method of organizing ideas for your particular topic, and it will make it easy to think of things to say and examples to present. Possible organizational patterns include:

- **Past-Present-Future** to describe how something once was, how it has changed, and how it will be in the future
- **Time** to describe chronological events or processes in sequential order
- **Problem-Solution** to describe a problem and ways to solve it
- **Location** to divide a topic into different geographical settings
- **Cause-Effect** to describe a situation and its effects
- **Effect-Cause** to describe a situation and its causes
- **Related Subtopics** to divide a topic into different parts
- **Advantage-Disadvantage** to describe positive and negative aspects of a topic

For detailed information about these patterns, review pages 76–77 of Chapter 5: Speaking to Inform.

Outlining the Impromptu Speech

When preparing for an impromptu speech, it can be helpful to create an outline for your ideas. This outline can be a real outline, which you write on paper, or a mental outline, which you keep in your head. When you create an outline, try to choose an organizational pattern that fits your topic. When Marco was asked to give an impromptu speech on "Addictions," he divided the topic into several parts. Notice how he used the pattern of related subtopics in the outline that follows.

Example: Marco's Outline

INTRODUCTION

I. I'll bet everyone in this room knows an addict! That's right, I said *addict*. Before you get angry, please let me explain.

II. When we hear the word *addiction*, we usually think of harmful substances like drugs or alcohol. We forget there are many other kinds of addictions. I'd now like to remind you of some.

BODY

I. Television addictions
   A. Soap operas
   B. Detective shows
   C. Sports
      1. Football
      2. Baseball
      3. Wrestling

II. Book addictions
   A. Romance novels
   B. Mysteries
   C. Science fiction

III. Eating addictions
   A. Ice cream
   B. Chocolate

IV. Other addictions
   A. Shopping
      1. Clothes
      2. CDs
      3. Antiques

B. Hobbies
   1. Stamp collecting
   2. Photography
C. Sports
   1. Golf
   2. Jogging
   3. Swimming

CONCLUSION

I. As you can see, not all addictions are bad for you. And, much to your surprise, you probably know someone who is an addict!

II. What kind of addict are you?

Activity

Discuss possible organizational patterns for speech topics.

1. Marco used the pattern of related subtopics to organize his speech on the topic of "Addictions." What other organizational patterns could be used for this topic?

   _____

2. What subtopics could be used for each organizational pattern?

   _____

   _____

   _____

   _____

3. What organizational patterns could be used for each of the following topics?

   a) Travel _____

   b) Culture shock _____

   c) Mercy killing _____

   d) Discrimination _____

   e) Capital punishment _____

   f) Child abuse _____

   g) Gambling _____

   h) Punctuality _____

i) Stress _____

j) Free speech _____

Guidelines for Impromptu Speaking

The following guidelines will help you relax and speak confidently when giving an impromptu speech:

1. Stay calm and begin slowly in order to give yourself time to think. No one is expecting a perfectly prepared speech. The audience knows this is an impromptu speech.

2. Begin with an attention-getting opener that is related to your talk. For example, make a startling statement, use a quotation from a well-known person, or ask the audience a question. Don't begin your speech with "My topic is X," or "Today I'm going to talk about X."

3. If you get confused or forget what you want to say, don't apologize to the audience. Stop briefly and organize your thoughts, and then continue speaking as if nothing happened.

4. Finish your speech gracefully with words your audience will remember. Don't end your speech with "I can't think of anything else" or "That's it." Review the information on page 81 of Chapter 5: Speaking to Inform and pages 103–104 of Chapter 6: Speaking to Persuade for hints about preparing memorable concluding remarks.

Assignment

Make an impromptu speech.

1. Your teacher may use the form on page 195 to evaluate your speech. Look it over so you know exactly how you will be evaluated.

2. Your teacher will give you an impromptu speech topic. Possible topics include those in question 3 of the Activity on pages 154–155. Think about how to develop and organize your speech for a few minutes. Your teacher may allow you to write your ideas on an index card.

3. Give a two to three minute speech about the topic.

[b], [v], AND [w]

A common error is to pronounce the sound [b] or [w] like [v], and vice versa. If you confuse [b] and [v], **vote** sounds like **boat** and **best** sounds like **vest**. If you confuse [w] and [v], **wine** sounds like **vine** and **vet** sounds like **wet**.

To pronounce [b], press your lips firmly together. To pronounce [v], place your top teeth over your bottom lip. To pronounce [w], round your lips and don't let your lower lip touch your upper teeth.

Exercise A

Read the following sets of words aloud. Be sure to press your lips together for [b], place your top teeth over your bottom lip for [v], and round your lips for [w].

	[b]	[v]	[w]
1.	**b**est	vest	west
2.	**b**et	vet	wet
3.	**B**arry	vary	wary
4.	**b**ent	vent	went
5.	**b**e	V	we

Exercise B

Read the following sentences aloud. Concentrate on pronouncing [b], [v], and [w] correctly.

1. A **whale would** look silly **wearing** a **veil**.
2. That **vest** is the **best** in the **west**.
3. The **berry** tastes **very sweet**.
4. The **vet** got **wet** in the rain.
5. She **bent** the metal **vent**.

Exercise C

Circle all words in the following poem that have the sound [v]. Then read the poem aloud. Be sure to place your top teeth over your bottom lip as you pronounce words with [v].

I Never Saw a Moor

I never saw a moor,
I never saw the sea;
Yet know I how the heather looks,
And what a wave must be.

I never spoke with God,
Nor visited in Heaven;
Yet certain am I of the spot
As if the chart were given.

—Emily Dickinson

Chapter 11

Using Idioms and Proverbs

Every language has popular expressions that don't always mean what one would expect. These popular expressions are known as *idioms*. An idiom cannot be translated literally. Attempts to do so often lead to confusion and frustration. For example, the English idiom *you're pulling my leg* means "You're kidding or not telling the truth." It doesn't really mean that you are holding my leg and pulling it.

Every language also has popular expressions that express advice or wisdom. These expressions are known as proverbs. For example, the English proverb *Don't look a gift horse in the mouth* means "Don't be critical of a gift. Accept it graciously."

Improving your ability to understand and use these expressions will help improve your speech communication skills. It will enable you to better understand your American friends and express yourself in a natural, informal manner.

In this chapter, you will learn and use a variety of idioms and proverbs.

Idioms with Body Parts

The following idioms include names of body parts.

1. **pull someone's leg:** to joke about something or exaggerate
   Are you *pulling my leg?* Tell me the truth!

2. **not have a leg to stand on:** to not have proof or support for an idea or decision
   Without a witness, you *don't have a leg to stand on.*

3. **on one's last legs:** in the last phase before collapse or death
   That horse doesn't look too strong. I think it's on *its last legs.*

4. **foot the bill:** to pay the expenses
   My father is *footing the bill* for my education.

5. **stand on one's own two feet:** to be independent or responsible for one's own life
   Now that you are twenty-one, you should *stand on your own two feet.*

6. **put one's foot down:** to take a firm stand
   My father *put his foot down* and said I couldn't use the car.

7. **put one's foot in one's mouth:** to say something embarrassing
   Think before you speak so you don't *put your foot in your mouth.*

8. **make one's mouth water:** to stimulate the appetite
   The smell of Mom's cooking *makes my mouth water.*

9. **melt in one's mouth:** to taste very good
   Grandmother's apple pie *melts in your mouth.*

10. **see eye to eye:** to agree completely
    We get along well because we usually *see eye to eye.*

11. **pull the wool over someone's eyes:** to deceive or trick someone
    My teacher didn't believe my excuse. I couldn't *pull the wool over her eyes.*

12. **butterflies in one's stomach:** a feeling of nervousness
    When I speak before large groups, I get *butterflies in my stomach.*

13. **over one's head:** too difficult to understand
    Stella can't understand the chapter; it's *over her head.*

14. **lose one's head:** to lose control
    After I got a small raise, I *lost my head* and bought an expensive car.

15. **out of hand:** out of control
    The poorly conducted meeting got *out of hand.*

16. **lend a hand:** to provide assistance
    I'll *lend a hand* and help you fix your car.

17. **one's heart is not in (something):** one is not interested or enthusiastic about (something)
    My heart's not in doing housework today.

18. **by heart:** so that it is memorized
    I know the "Pledge of Allegiance" *by heart.*

19. **slap in the face:** an insult
    John called me stupid. That's a real *slap in the face.*

20. **elbow room:** space to move around
    My kitchen is too small. There is no *elbow room.*

21. **hold one's tongue:** to keep quiet
    Please *hold your tongue*—I don't want to hear about it.

22. **wet behind the ears:** having very little experience
    He's not ready to be the boss; he's still *wet behind the ears.*

23. **all ears:** willing to listen carefully
    Tell me what is bothering you—I'm *all ears.*

24. **cross one's fingers:** to wish for good luck or success
    I'll *cross my fingers* that you'll win the race.

25. **on the nose:** exact
    Your answer to that question was right *on the nose.*

Exercise A

Write the letter of the sentence that best shows the meaning of the idiom in italics.

_____ 1. José doesn't *stand on his own two feet*.
  a) He prefers to sit on a chair.
  b) He broke a leg and can't stand up.
  c) He always asks others to help him.

_____ 2. Chocolate *makes my mouth water*.
  a) It makes me hungry.
  b) It makes me thirsty.
  c) It takes away my hunger.

_____ 3. This is getting *out of hand*.
  a) This fell out of my hand.
  b) I burned my hand.
  c) The situation is out of control.

_____ 4. That was a *slap in the face*.
  a) Someone hit me in the face.
  b) Someone insulted me.
  c) Someone complimented me.

_____ 5. Ali is *in over his head*.
  a) He is underwater.
  b) He is very short.
  c) He can't handle the work.

_____ 6. Susanna is *wet behind the ears*.
  a) She didn't dry her ears.
  b) She doesn't have much experience.
  c) She hears well.

_____ 7. Kim doesn't know when to *hold his tongue*.
  a) He always tells important secrets.
  b) He can't roll his tongue up.
  c) He always sticks his tongue out when he is angry.

_____ 8. They don't *see eye to eye*.
  a) They never look at each other.
  b) They always wear dark sunglasses.
  c) They don't agree with each other.

_____ 9. That car is *on its last legs*.

       a) It only has one tire.

       b) It needs a paint job.

       c) It is about to break down completely.

_____ 10. You got it *right on the nose*.

       a) It hit your nose.

       b) It fits your nose perfectly.

       c) You did it perfectly.

Exercise B

Match each idiom with its meaning.

_____ 1. butterflies in one's stomach	a)	a nervous feeling
_____ 2. foot the bill	b)	to deceive someone
_____ 3. by heart	c)	to be uninterested
_____ 4. pull the wool over someone's eyes	d)	to pay the costs
_____ 5. not have one's heart in it	e)	by memory
_____ 6. lose one's head	f)	to help out
_____ 7. elbow room	g)	to take a firm stand
_____ 8. cross one's fingers	h)	to act foolishly
_____ 9. lend a hand	i)	to wish for good luck
_____ 10. put one's foot down	j)	space to move

Idioms with Foods

The following idioms include names of foods.

1. **as easy as pie:** very easy to do
   A child could do it; it's *as easy as pie*.

2. **a piece of cake:** very easy to do
   I can fix your car in ten minutes. It's *a piece of cake!*

3. **spill the beans:** to tell a secret
   Pierre *spilled the beans* and told me about the surprise party.

4. **like sardines (in a can):** very crowded
   In Tokyo, people pack into the subway *like sardines in a can*.

5. **cry over spilled milk:** to worry about something that has already happened

   You lost your ring a year ago. Don't *cry over spilled milk.*

6. **the cream of the crop:** the best people

   The students who get admitted to that school are really *the cream of the crop.*

7. **lemon:** a product with many defects

   This new car is a *lemon*; nothing works right.

8. **fishy:** seeming wrong or suspicious

   There is something *fishy* about his story; I don't believe it.

9. **as cool as a cucumber:** having much self-confidence and self-control

   The president is *as cool as a cucumber,* even under pressure.

10. **hot potato:** a controversial topic

    The subject of capital punishment is a *hot potato.*

Exercise

Circle the letter of the phrase that correctly explains the meaning of the idiom.

1. spill the beans
   a) to drop vegetables
   b) to tell a secret
   c) to keep a secret

2. a piece of cake
   a) something difficult
   b) a portion of dessert
   c) something very simple

3. fishy
   a) like tuna
   b) right
   c) wrong

4. as easy as pie
   a) easy to bake
   b) easy to do
   c) easy to eat

5. cry over spilled milk
   a) to complain about something in the past
   b) to cry because there's no food
   c) to complain about an unfair situation

6. hot potato
   a) a controversial topic
   b) a person who gets angry easily
   c) a potato that isn't cold

7. like sardines (in a can)
   a) like something sold in supermarkets
   b) very crowded
   c) identical

8. the cream of the crop
   a) something grown on a farm
   b) dairy products
   c) the best people

9. as cool as a cucumber
   a) very self-assured
   b) very cool
   c) lukewarm

10. lemon
   a) a yellow citrus fruit
   b) something that requires much work
   c) a defective product

Idioms with Colors

The following idioms include names of colors.

1. **green with envy:** very jealous
   When I won the prize, all my friends were *green with envy*.

2. **blue:** sad
   He is feeling *blue* because his dog died.

3. **scared yellow:** very afraid
   She saw a ghost and was *scared yellow*.

4. **see red:** to be very angry
   My father *saw red* when I broke his new radio.

5. **rosy:** favorable; bright
   Ricardo just inherited a lot of money; his future looks *rosy*.

6. **green:** lacking experience
   She needs more training; she's still *green*.

7. **in the red:** in debt
   His business is *in the red*.

8. **in the pink:** in good health
   My doctor told me I was *in the pink*.

9. **out of the blue:** unexpectedly

   I hadn't heard from my uncle in fifteen years. Yesterday, he called me *out of the blue*.

10. **white lie:** a lie that is not serious; a fib

    The woman told a *white lie*. She said her hair was naturally blonde.

Exercise

Write the idiom associated with each word.

1. jealous _____
2. afraid _____
3. unhappy _____
4. healthy _____
5. in debt _____

6. good _____
7. unexpectedly _____
8. angry _____
9. inexperienced _____
10. untruth _____

Miscellaneous Idioms

The following idioms are about a variety of topics.

1. **under the weather:** ill

   Randy isn't going to the party; he's a bit *under the weather*.

2. **throw in the towel:** to give up

   Don't *throw in the towel*; finish your education.

3. **put the cart before the horse:** to reverse the correct order of events

   I *put the cart before the horse* and bought a car before I learned how to drive.

4. **make tracks:** to move fast

   Let's *make tracks* and stop wasting time.

5. **put two and two together:** to reach a conclusion

   We *put two and two together* and realized why our mother was angry.

6. **get to the point:** to come to the important part of one's message

   I'm very busy. Please *get to the point*.

7. **beat around the bush:** to speak vaguely or indirectly

   Stop *beating around the bush* and get to the point.

8. **run in the family:** to be characteristic of family members
   All my sisters are tall; height *runs in my family.*

9. **eat one's words:** to take back what one said
   When I learned I was wrong, I had to *eat my words.*

10. **square away:** to finish; to put in order or solve
    The deal is *squared away* now that all the papers
    have been sent.

11. **pull (some/a few) strings:** to use influence; to manipulate
    You're the boss's son. Can you please *pull some strings*
    and get me a job?

12. **face the music:** to accept the consequences of one's actions
    The criminal had to *face the music* in the courtroom.

Exercise A

Substitute one of the following idioms for the italicized words in each
sentence. Be sure to use the correct grammatical form of each idiom.

put two and two together	face the music
put the cart before the horse	make tracks
under the weather	square away
get to the point	eat one's words
run in the family	throw in the towel
pull (some/a few) strings	

Example: I used my father's boat without permission; now I am ready
to *be punished.* face the music

1. The police *solved the mystery* and caught the thief.

   _____

2. You don't have much time; *be specific* and explain yourself clearly.

   _____

3. Carl called me a bad cardplayer. He had to *take back what he said*
   when I won every game. _____

4. The teacher told the students to *work faster* and finish their
   assignment. _____

5. Helga was discouraged and *gave up.* She dropped out of school.

   _____

6. Bill caught the flu. He's *not feeling well.*

   _____

7. All the problems with my car *have* finally *been taken care of.*

   _____

8. Blonde hair *is a common trait in my family.* My mother and three sisters are all blondes. _____

9. I'd like to be an actress. Do you know any people who could *use their influence* and get me a part in a movie?

   _____

10. Elena planned a big party for Linda without first finding out if Linda could come. Elena always *does things backwards.*

    _____

Exercise B

Finish each sentence with a phrase that shows an understanding of the idiomatic expression in italics. Be sure to use correct grammar and sentence structure.

Examples

a) The meeting got *out of hand* when everyone started shouting and throwing papers.

b) Good looks and intelligence *run in my family.*

c) We don't always *see eye to eye* but we are very good friends.

1. I finally *put two and two together* and _____.

2. I feel *blue* when _____.

3. His car is a *lemon* because _____.

4. _____ *like sardines in a can.*

5. He *threw in the towel* when _____.

6. Sue *spilled the beans* by _____.

7. I think *her heart's not in her work* because _____.

8. My friend was *green with envy* when _____.

9. Maria *put the cart before the horse* and _____.

10. _____ *on the nose.*

11. It's time to *put your foot down* and _____.

12. I get *butterflies in my stomach* when _____.

13. The students got *out of hand* when _____.

14. _____ *makes my mouth water.*

15. I'll try to *pull some strings* and _____.

16. My mother *saw red* when _____.

17. I tried to *pull the wool over her eyes* by _____.

18. Julio had to *eat his words* after _____.

19. Elena was feeling *under the weather* because

_____.

20. For me, _____ is *as easy as pie.*

21. His story that _____ sounds *fishy.*

22. Please *lend a hand* and _____.

23. Let's *make tracks* and _____.

24. My parents aren't willing to *foot the bill* for

_____.

25. I know _____ *by heart.*

26. He *put his foot in his mouth* when _____.

Proverbs

Every language has proverbs or sayings that express advice or wisdom. You may already be familiar with some English proverbs. For example, the proverb *Let sleeping dogs lie* means "Don't bother something or someone if the person or thing is not bothering you."

Improving your ability to understand and to use these expressions will help improve your speech communication skills.

Activity

Try to find the meaning of each proverb below. Ask anyone who is willing to help you. If possible, write a proverb from your native language that has a similar meaning. Come to class prepared to discuss the expressions.

1. A stitch in time saves nine.

2. An ounce of prevention is worth a pound of cure.

3. A watched pot never boils.

4. The grass is always greener on the other side.

5. When in Rome, do as the Romans do.

6. When the cat's away, the mice will play.

7. People who live in glass houses shouldn't throw stones.

8. A bird in the hand is worth two in the bush.

9. Don't put all your eggs in one basket.

10. Don't count your chickens before they hatch.

11. Look before you leap.

12. A rolling stone gathers no moss.

13. All that glitters is not gold.

14. It's useless to lock the stable door after the horse has bolted.

15. Birds of a feather flock together.

16. Old houses mended cost little less than new before they're ended.

17. You can't judge a book by its cover.

18. Cross each bridge as you come to it.

19. It's easier to catch flies with honey than vinegar.

20. Half a loaf is better than none.

21. Strike while the iron is hot.

22. Give him an inch and he'll take a mile.

23. That's like borrowing from Peter to pay Paul.

24. The pot is calling the kettle black.

25. Too many cooks spoil the broth.

Assignment

Make a speech about an idiom or a proverb.

1. Choose an idiom or a proverb.

2. Prepare notes for a presentation about the idiom or proverb. Include the following components:
   - an attention-getting opener
   - a clear statement of the idiom or expression
   - an explanation of the idiom or expression's general meaning
   - two examples that illustrate the idiom or expression's meaning
   - a graceful conclusion

3. Your teacher may use the form on page 196 to evaluate your speech. Look it over so you know exactly how you will be evaluated.

4. Give a two to three minute speech about the idiom or proverb.

 Example

ATTENTION-GETTING OPENER

What would you do if your parents went on vacation and left you home alone? Would you stay out late? Would you throw wild parties and invite all your friends? I'm sure no one here would act so irresponsibly, but there are plenty of people who would!

CLEAR STATEMENT OF IDIOM OR PROVERB

Many of you have heard the expression "When the cat's away, the mice will play."

EXPLANATION

This saying means that animals or people might take advantage of a situation and behave poorly if no one is there to supervise.

EXAMPLE A

For example, I left my two dogs at home alone while I went to the store. When I returned, I saw that they had chewed a hole in the carpet. This would not have happened if someone had stayed home to watch them.

EXAMPLE B

Another example happened when my teacher was giving our class a test. He left the classroom for a few minutes. When he came back into the room, everyone was talking and telling each other the answers. If he had stayed in the room, the students could not have cheated.

GRACEFUL CONCLUSION

My brother was complaining that whenever he goes out of town, his employees come in late, leave early, and don't do their work. I told him, "You know what they say, 'When the cat's away, the mice will play!'"

INTONATION

Intonation refers to the use of melody and the rise and fall of the voice when speaking. It can determine grammatical meaning as well as the speaker's attitude. Correct use of intonation will convey your message effectively and help you sound like a native English speaker.

Intonation should **fall** (↘) at the end of declarative statements or information questions.

Examples

I like school. ↘
She is kind. ↘
Where is it? ↘
Why should I do it? ↘

Intonation should **rise** (↗) at the end of statements expressing doubt or yes/no questions.

Examples

I got an A? ↗
You ate twenty-five hot dogs? ↗
Will he stay? ↗
Did it rain? ↗

 Exercise A

Read each of the following statements twice. First use falling intonation, and then use rising intonation. Notice how the falling intonation makes you sound certain, while rising intonation makes you sound uncertain.

Stated with Certainty ↘	Stated with Doubt ↗
1. You ran fifty-five miles.	You ran fifty-five miles?
2. He drank eight gallons of wine.	He drank eight gallons of wine?
3. She lifted five hundred pounds.	She lifted five hundred pounds?
4. They have twenty children.	They have twenty children?

Exercise B

With a partner, practice reading the following yes/no questions and responses aloud. Be sure your intonation rises at the end of each question and falls at the end of each response.

Questions ↗	Responses ↘
1. Can you see?	Yes, I can.
2. Are we leaving?	No, we're staying.
3. May I help you?	Yes, please do.
4. Is Sue your sister?	No, she's my friend.
5. Did he arrive?	Yes, he's here now.

Exercise C

Read the following statements and questions aloud. Next to each sentence, draw an upward arrow if rising intonation is used and a downward arrow if falling intonation is used.

Example

Can you sing? __↗__

1. I feel fine. _____

2. When's your birthday? _____

3. Did you see my friend? _____

4. Why did Tom leave? _____

5. We like to travel. _____

Chapter 12

Miscellaneous Speaking Activities

By now you have probably given several speeches to your classmates. In the process, you have improved your self-confidence and ability to speak before a group. You have learned how to research, organize, prepare, and deliver a variety of speeches. You have also improved your listening skills, understanding of interpersonal and intercultural communication, and ability to use idioms and other expressions.

In this chapter, you will draw on the skills you have learned in previous chapters. You will find suggestions for conducting a variety of fun and educational speech-communication activities, including a symposium, interpersonal/intercultural activity, debate, speaker introduction, progressive story, and personal opinion speech.

Symposium

A *symposium* is a group presentation that generally consists of five or six participants. Each participant gives a short speech focusing on a different aspect of the same topic.

In preparation for the symposium, the participants select a group leader. Next, they choose a general topic that is of interest to all. Then, they establish the purpose of the symposium, which could be to inform, to persuade, or to solve a problem. After brainstorming and evaluating possible subtopics, each participant chooses one. Each participant prepares for his or her part of the symposium. (Detailed guidelines on how to prepare for informative speeches are in Chapter 5: Speaking to Inform. Guidelines on how to prepare for persuasive speech are in Chapter 6: Speaking to Persuade. Guidelines on how to prepare for problem-solving group discussions are in Chapter 7: Participating in Group Discussions.) Finally, they deliver the symposium.

The group leader has additional responsiblities. At the beginning of the symposium, he or she introduces the participants, provides an attention-getting opener, and previews the subtopics to be covered. During the symposium, the group leader provides a transition between each speaker's presentation, and at the end of the symposium, he or she summarizes the subtopics discussed, concludes the symposium gracefully, thanks the audience and the participants, and leads a question-and-answer session. Audience members may direct questions to the entire group or to specific participants.

Assignment

Conduct a symposium on a topic of your choice.

1. Choose a leader for your group.

2. Choose a general topic that interests all group members and can be researched easily.

3. Determine the purpose of the symposium (informative, persuasive, or problem-solving).

4. Brainstorm possible subtopics.

5. Choose the best subtopics and assign one to each participant.

6. On your own, prepare for your part of the symposium.

7. Present the symposium.

Interpersonal/Intercultural Activity

We all have beliefs—some correct, others incorrect—about other people and other cultures. In Chapter 8: Understanding Interpersonal Communication, you learned how to improve interpersonal communication and how to avoid misunderstandings. In Chapter 9: Understanding Intercultural Communication, you learned how beliefs, values, and behavioral patterns differ across cultures and how these differences may affect intercultural communication.

This activity will enable you to better understand and appreciate the different personal and cultural values of your classmates.

Assignment

1. Before class, select a coin from your country that you think best represents you as a person. Possible reasons for choosing the coin might be its:

value	size	shape
color	inscription	picture

2. Bring the coin to class. In a circle with your classmates, explain your reasons for selecting the coin.

3. Select the classmate to whom you would most like to give the coin. Possible reasons for choosing a classmate might be:

   - admiration for the person
   - a feeling that you are very similar to that person
   - a feeling that you are very different from that person and a wish to better understand him or her
   - a desire to encourage that person
   - a desire that the person change something about himself or herself
   - something about the coin reminds you of the person

4. Give your coin to the person you chose in Step 3. Do this one student at a time, without speaking, until all students have given away their original coins.

5. Explain your reason for giving your coin to the recipient.

6. Discuss the following questions:

   a) How did you feel if you received coins?

   b) How did you feel if you didn't receive any coins?

   c) Why do you think you received or didn't receive any coins?

d) Can you think of any situations in life that are similar to this exercise?

e) What have you learned about your classmates from this exercise?

f) What have you learned about other cultures from this exercise?

Debate

A *debate* is a speaking situation in which opposite points of view are presented and argued. Each speaker attempts to convince the audience to agree with his or her ideas. A debate thus consists of two opposing persuasive speeches. A debate can be between two speakers or two teams. In a debate between two speakers, Speaker A speaks in favor of the topic or proposition being debated; Speaker B speaks against the topic or proposition. The speakers take turns giving main speeches and rebuttals. In the main speeches, the speakers focus on presenting evidence to convince the audience to agree with them. In the rebuttals, they focus on attacking the opponent's position and trying to disprove his or her evidence. When the speakers have finished, the audience decides which speaker has won the debate.

Before the debate, each pair of opponents decides on the topic to be debated. Then, they form a *proposition,* or a statement that can be argued. They then decide who will speak in favor of the proposition (Speaker A) and who will argue against it (Speaker B). Possible debate topics follow:

- Highway speed limits should be lowered.
- Hitchhiking should be legal.
- Students caught cheating should be expelled.
- Capital punishment should be abolished.
- The government should impose rent controls on landlords.
- Required courses in college should be abolished.
- Prostitution is not immoral.
- Tuition fees for international students are too high.

The remaining steps in preparing for the debate are similar to the steps in preparing for a persuasive speech. Each speaker analyzes the audience, gathers information, and organizes his or her speech. For detailed information about how to prepare for persuasive speeches, review Chapter 6: Speaking to Persuade.

Assignment

Conduct a debate on a topic of your choice.

1. With your opponent, choose a topic.

2. Form a proposition. Decide who will speak in favor of the proposition (Speaker A), and who will speak against the proposition (Speaker B).

3. On your own, prepare for the debate. Analyze the audience, gather information, and organize your speech.

4. Conduct the debate as follows:

   a) Speaker A gives his or her main speech for four minutes. He or she introduces, defines or explains, establishes, and provides evidence for the proposition.

   b) Speaker B gives a rebuttal for four minutes. He or she summarizes his or her disagreement with Speaker A's information. Speaker B then gives his or her main speech for four minutes. He or she disagrees with Speaker A's proposition, provides evidence, and summarizes his or her own view.

   c) Speaker A gives a rebuttal for four minutes. He or she restates his or her original points, restates and tries to disprove Speaker B's argument, reemphasizes his or her original argument and provides more evidence, and restates his or her original proposition.

5. The audience votes for the best speaker.

Example: Outline for Debate on Topic "Used-Car Salesmen Are Dishonest"

SPEAKER A: MAIN SPEECH

I. *Introduces the proposition and clearly defines or explains it*:
   A. Defines *used-car salesman*
   B. Defines *dishonest*

II. *Establishes the problem*: Most used-car salesmen will cheat you if they can.
   A. My friend lost $500 when he sold his car last year. The salesman told him it was worth $1,000 on a trade-in. He could have sold it himself for $1,500.
   B. A used-car salesman didn't tell my friend that the dealership wouldn't service the car after he bought it. This was explained in the contract in very fine print that no one could see.
   C. A used-car salesman never mentions that the car you want has a history of mechanical problems.

III. *Summarizes the affirmative view*: In summary, most used-car salesmen are dishonest.
   A. People lose hundreds or thousands of dollars when they buy or sell cars through used-car dealerships.
   B. Used-car salesmen are known to tell lies to convince you to buy an old car.

SPEAKER B: REBUTTAL & MAIN SPEECH

I. *Summarizes his or her disagreement with the affirmative speaker's information*:
   A. *Accepts or rejects the other speaker's explanation or definition of the proposition.*
   B. *Disagrees with the opponent's arguments*: I disagree completely with what my opponent just presented:
      1. That used-car salesmen want you to lose money
      2. That used-car salesmen tell you lies
II. *Disagrees with the proposition*: Used-car salesmen do not purposely try to cheat people.
   A. I'll admit some people lose money, but it is their own fault, not the salesman's. Car dealers are in business to make a profit. They will pay you a fair price for your car. If you think it is worth more, you should try to sell it on your own.
   B. A used-car salesman doesn't force anyone to sign a contract without reading it. The first speaker's friend should not have signed anything without reading it. If he had looked at the contract more closely, he would have known the dealership wouldn't service the car.
   C. There is no rule that a salesman must volunteer information about a car's problems.
      1. A salesman may use "omission." He doesn't have to supply information if you don't ask for it. It's the buyer's responsibility to ask specific questions about possible problems.
      2. A buyer must do his or her homework and not rely on a salesperson to supply all the information. A buyer who doesn't do this is like an ostrich with his head buried in the sand!
III. *Summarizes the negative view*: In summary, used-car salesmen are as honest as any group of sales professionals.
   A. A salesman is in business to make as much money as he can.
   B. A businessman would be crazy to say, "That's too much profit for me, you should pay less money!"

C. People must think and argue for themselves. It's our own responsibility to learn to get the best deal we can when we buy or sell a used car. If we don't, it's our own fault.

SPEAKER A: REBUTTAL

I. *Restates original points*: The facts I presented in my opening speech still hold. I stated that:
   A. Most used-car salesman are dishonest.
   B. They will cheat you if they can.
   C. They will tell lies to convince you to buy an old car.

II. *Restates and tries to disprove Speaker B's argument*: The negative speaker tried but could not prove me wrong.
   A. The negative speaker gave no evidence or examples to prove used-car salesmen do not purposely cheat people.
   B. The negative speaker claims it was my friend's responsibility to read the fine print in the contract.
      1. If the contract had been honest, it would have been easy to read.
      2. If the contract had been honest, it would have been in large print.
   C. The other speaker claims a salesman may use omission.
      1. A deliberate omission is a lie!
      2. The average buyer can't know everything about every car.

III. *Reemphasizes original argument and provides more evidence*: I know of two other people in this school who have been cheated by used-car salesmen.
   A. Humberto's experience
   B. Ulrich's experience

IV. *Restates original proposition*: In summary, the negative speaker did not prove me wrong.
   A. Used-car salesmen are dishonest.
   B. Please vote for the affirmative side of the proposition.

Introductory Speech

In an *introductory speech,* a person introduces a guest speaker to the audience. This type of speech has several purposes:
- to acquaint the audience with the guest speaker
- to make the speaker comfortable

- to interest the audience in the speaker and his or her topic
- to announce the topic
- to give the speaker's name

A good introductory speech is short, preferably two minutes or less. To create a short, effective introductory speech, use the T.I.S. method, which is based on Dale Carnegie's approach to public speaking. Introduce the

- **Topic:** Announce the topic to be discussed and the title of the speech.
- **Importance of the topic:** Explain why the topic is important to the audience and why they will be particularly interested in it.
- **Speaker:** Explain why the speaker is qualified to talk about this topic. Relevant background information might include the speaker's education, special honors, special training, professional experience, club memberships, or travel experience. The final words of your introduction should be the speaker's name. Be sure to pronounce it correctly and clearly.

 Example

TOPIC

Our speaker today is going to talk about why small businesses fail.

IMPORTANCE OF TOPIC

Since this audience is composed mainly of business majors, you will find our speaker's information quite valuable. As many of you are planning to open your own business after graduation or to help run the family business, it is very important to learn how to prevent this problem from happening. You should be most eager to hear what our guest has to say.

SPEAKER

Our speaker today has studied business law and administration in Venezuela. He has a degree in business administration from the University of Caracas and graduated with honors. He is currently majoring in accounting at our university and is the president of the accounting society on campus. Our speaker helped supervise his father's import/export company for five years. As you can see, he is most qualified to speak on the topic. It is with great pleasure that I now introduce to you, Mr. Carlos Alvarez.

Assignment

Your assignment is to introduce a real or imaginary speaker to your classmates.

1. Choose a guest speaker. Possible guest speakers include:

   a movie star   a scientist   a historical figure

   an artist   an inventor   a character from a book

   a political leader   an explorer   a classmate

2. Choose a topic for the speaker.

3. Give a one to two minute speech introducing the speaker.

Progressive Story

The *progressive story* is a fun, informal classroom speaking activity that encourages you to think on your feet and use your imagination. One person starts a story. He or she then calls on another person to continue the story. That person calls on one last person to conclude the story.

 Example

SPEAKER A

My best friend called one Saturday to ask if I would like to do two really fun things. First, take a drive in his new sports car. Second, go boating at the end of our drive. I said, "Sure!" It was a beautiful sunny day and we were driving with the sunroof open. The sun was shining and a cool breeze was blowing. We talked about how great the sailing would be when we got his sailboat out on the ocean. Then, without warning, something happened …

SPEAKER B

What happened was that a highway patrolman stopped the car that my friend and I were driving. The patrol car pulled alongside of us and pointed to the side of the road. We did not know what we had done wrong because we were driving at the legal speed limit. After we were pulled over, the trooper told us that the trailer with the boat had no taillight. The trooper then became suspicious of us—probably because my friend was Colombian. He searched our car and boat and found two burlap bags in the back of the car. The trooper asked us what the bags contained and we told him that …

SPEAKER C

The two burlap bags contained Colombian coffee. My friend had just arrived two days before from a visit to Bogotá, Colombia. His father owned a large coffee exporting company in the country. The policeman didn't believe us. He took us to the police station. They took our coffee away from us and said it had to be tested. Finally, after realizing that we had done nothing wrong, they gave us back the coffee and let us go.

We never did go sailing that day, but we did learn a new lesson about living in America. Never, never carry your coffee in a burlap bag that says "Colombian" on the side!

Assignment

In groups of three, create a progressive story.

1. Before class, prepare a one-minute introduction to a short story. Possible topics include:

an experience	a pet peeve	a fairy tale
an activity	an argument	a dream

2. In class, Speaker A begins a story and speaks for one minute. Speaker A then calls on Speaker B.

3. Speaker B continues Speaker A's story for one minute. Speaker B then calls on Speaker C.

4. Speaker C speaks for one minute, continuing and concluding Speaker B's story.

Personal Opinion Speech

A *personal opinion speech* expresses the speaker's attitude and feelings about a topic. The feelings could be positive, such as enthusiasm or excitement, or negative, such as anger or worry. The topic could be an issue, policy, situation, attitude, or behavior. Topics that people feel strongly about include:

Cruelty to animals	Learning a second language
Child abuse	Punishing criminals
World peace	Children
Drunk drivers	Dishonesty
Drugs	Rudeness
Their city	Their school

In the introduction of a personal opinion speech, the speaker gives a clear statement of his or her opinion. In the body, the speaker explains the reasons for his or her opinion and gives at least one example. In the conclusion, the speaker restates the opinion and offers advice. Note that in personal opinion speeches it is especially effective for the speaker to use emotion so that the audience can empathize with his or her feelings.

 **Example**

INTRODUCTION

The other day I heard an American student say, "All foreign students are the same! They can't understand me and I can't understand them." This comment bothered me. In my opinion, American students should give other people a chance and not assume all students from other countries are alike.

BODY

I believe that all people are unique. We all look different, we like different foods, some of us are shy and some are brave, and we all have different good and bad qualities. I say that just because we don't speak perfect English yet, all foreign students are not the same. I may be from another country but I understand what Americans say, and every day I'm learning to speak English much better. People should not jump to conclusions about other people. We all must learn to be patient and give each person a chance.

CONCLUSION

Foreign students cannot be lumped together and called the same. American students are not all the same either. We are all different and we all have our own problems to face and solve. We must learn to be more patient with one another and realize that no one is perfect. That's my opinion!

Assignment

Your assignment is to give a speech expressing your opinion about a topic.

1. Choose a topic that you feel strongly about.

2. Prepare notes for a speech about your opinion. Be sure to include your opinion, your reasons for your opinion, and at least one example.

3. Give a two to three minute speech about your opinion.

Pronunciation Tip

[l] AND [r]

Some students confuse the sounds [l] and [r]. If they confuse these sounds, **rice** sounds like **lice**, and **berry** sounds like **belly**.

Pronounce [l] by placing the tip of your tongue against the gum ridge just behind your upper front teeth. Pronounce [r] by curling your tongue upward but not letting it touch the roof of your mouth.

Exercise A

Read the following pairs of words and sentences aloud. Concentrate on pronouncing [l] and [r] correctly.

[l]	[r]
1. **l**ate	**r**ate
2. **l**ed	**r**ed
3. e**l**ect	e**r**ect
4. Move toward the **light**.	Move toward the **right**.
5. It was very **long**.	It was very **wrong**.
6. Please **collect** the papers.	Please **correct** the papers.

Exercise B

Read the following sentences aloud. Concentrate on pronouncing [l] and [r] correctly.

1. Carry that **load** down the **road**.
2. We saw a **palace** in **Paris**.
3. I left the **rake** near the **lake**.
4. He **lied** about the long **ride**.
5. **Jerry** likes **jelly** doughnuts.

Exercise C

Read the following pairs of words and sentences aloud. Concentrate on pronouncing the consonant blend at the beginning of each word smoothly. Be careful not to insert a vowel between consonants.

Example

Word Pair:	**bl**oom	**br**oom
Correct Pronunciation:	[blum]	[brum]
Incorrect Pronunciation:	[bəlum]	[bərum]

[l]	**[r]**
1. **pl**ay	**pr**ay
2. **cl**ue	**cr**ew
3. **gl**ow	**gr**ow
4. **fl**ock	**fr**ock
5. **cl**ash	**cr**ash

6. We had a **fright** on that **flight**.

7. That **brand** of food is **bland**.

8. Did **Blake break** his leg?

9. The **crew** had no **clue** of the storm.

10. **Fred fled** from the room.

Evaluation Forms

Personal Experience/Specific Fear Speech

Speaker _____ Topic _____ Date _____

DELIVERY	RATING	COMMENTS
Eye Contact	1 2 3 4 5	_____
Volume of Voice	1 2 3 4 5	_____
Rate of Speech	1 2 3 4 5	_____
Posture	1 2 3 4 5	_____
Adherence to Time Limit	1 2 3 4 5	_____

CONTENT	RATING	COMMENTS
Evidence of Preparation	1 2 3 4 5	_____
Introduction	1 2 3 4 5	_____
Choice of Topic	1 2 3 4 5	_____
Sufficient Use of Details	1 2 3 4 5	_____
Organization	1 2 3 4 5	_____
Conclusion	1 2 3 4 5	_____

ADDITIONAL COMMENTS

_____

_____

RATING KEY

1 = Poor   2 = Fair   3 = Acceptable   4 = Good   5 = Excellent

Meaningful Object Speech

Speaker _____ Object _____ Date _____

DELIVERY	RATING	COMMENTS
Eye Contact	1 2 3 4 5	_____
Volume of Voice	1 2 3 4 5	_____
Rate of Speech	1 2 3 4 5	_____
Enthusiasm	1 2 3 4 5	_____
Adherence to Time Limit	1 2 3 4 5	_____

CONTENT	RATING	COMMENTS
Evidence of Preparation	1 2 3 4 5	_____
Introduction	1 2 3 4 5	_____
Choice of Object	1 2 3 4 5	_____
Objective Information	1 2 3 4 5	_____
Subjective Information	1 2 3 4 5	_____
Organization	1 2 3 4 5	_____
Conclusion	1 2 3 4 5	_____

ADDITIONAL COMMENTS

_____

_____

RATING KEY

1 = Poor   2 = Fair   3 = Acceptable   4 = Good   5 = Excellent

Informative Speech

Speaker _____ Topic _____ Date _____

DELIVERY	RATING	COMMENTS
Eye Contact	1 2 3 4 5	_____
Volume of Voice	1 2 3 4 5	_____
Rate of Speech	1 2 3 4 5	_____
Enthusiasm	1 2 3 4 5	_____
Adherence to Time Limit	1 2 3 4 5	_____

CONTENT	RATING	COMMENTS
Attention-Getting Opener	1 2 3 4 5	_____
Preview	1 2 3 4 5	_____
Organization	1 2 3 4 5	_____
Supporting Materials	1 2 3 4 5	_____
Visual Aids	1 2 3 4 5	_____
Transitions	1 2 3 4 5	_____
Summary	1 2 3 4 5	_____
Concluding Remarks	1 2 3 4 5	_____

ADDITIONAL COMMENTS

_____

_____

RATING KEY

1 = Poor   2 = Fair   3 = Acceptable   4 = Good   5 = Excellent

Persuasive Speech

Speaker _____ Topic _____ Date _____

Persuasive Claim _____

DELIVERY	RATING	COMMENTS
Eye Contact	1 2 3 4 5	_____
Volume of Voice	1 2 3 4 5	_____
Rate of Speech	1 2 3 4 5	_____
Enthusiasm	1 2 3 4 5	_____
Adherence to Time Limit	1 2 3 4 5	_____

CONTENT	RATING	COMMENTS
Introduction	1 2 3 4 5	_____
Statement of Purpose	1 2 3 4 5	_____
Organization	1 2 3 4 5	_____
Supporting Evidence	1 2 3 4 5	_____
Visual Aids	1 2 3 4 5	_____
Transitions	1 2 3 4 5	_____
Summary	1 2 3 4 5	_____
Concluding Remarks	1 2 3 4 5	_____

ADDITIONAL COMMENTS

_____

_____

RATING KEY

1 = Poor   2 = Fair   3 = Acceptable   4 = Good   5 = Excellent

Group Discussion: Individual Participant

Participant _____ Problem _____ Date _____

PREPARATION	RATING	COMMENTS

Evidence of Planning   1 2 3 4 5   _____

Evidence of Research   1 2 3 4 5   _____

PARTICIPATION	RATING	COMMENTS

Sufficiency of Contributions   1 2 3 4 5   _____

Value of Contributions   1 2 3 4 5   _____

Adherence to Organizational Plan   1 2 3 4 5   _____

Respect for Others' Opinions   1 2 3 4 5   _____

ADDITIONAL COMMENTS

_____

_____

_____

_____

RATING KEY

1 = Poor   2 = Fair   3 = Acceptable   4 = Good   5 = Excellent

Group Discussion: Group Leader

Leader _____ Problem _____ Date _____

EFFECTIVENESS	RATING	COMMENTS

**Introduction
of Participants**   1 2 3 4 5   _____

**Introduction
of Problem**   1 2 3 4 5   _____

**Knowledge
of Topic**   1 2 3 4 5   _____

**Ability to Manage
Organizational Plan** 1 2 3 4 5   _____

**Ability to Encourage
Participation**   1 2 3 4 5   _____

**Ability to Handle
Conflicts**   1 2 3 4 5 n/a   _____

**Transitions
Between Steps**   1 2 3 4 5   _____

**Graceful
Conclusion**   1 2 3 4 5   _____

ADDITIONAL COMMENTS

_____

_____

_____

_____

RATING KEY

1 = Poor   2 = Fair   3 = Acceptable   4 = Good   5 = Excellent

Group Discussion: All Participants

Participants _____

Problem _____ Date _____

GROUP DYNAMICS   RATING   COMMENTS

1. **Participants freely
   expressed their opinions.**   1 2 3 4 5   _____

2. **The group stayed on topic.**   1 2 3 4 5   _____

3. **All members participated
   equally.**   1 2 3 4 5   _____

ORGANIZATION   RATING   COMMENTS

1. **The problem was
   clearly identified.**   1 2 3 4 5   _____

2. **The existence of the
   problem was proven.**   1 2 3 4 5   _____

3. **The causes of the problem
   were explained.**   1 2 3 4 5   _____

4. **Possible future effects
   of the problem were
   presented.**   1 2 3 4 5   _____

5. **Possible solutions
   were proposed.**   1 2 3 4 5   _____

6. **The best solutions
   were chosen.**   1 2 3 4 5   _____

ADDITIONAL COMMENTS

_____

_____

_____

_____

RATING KEY

1 = Poor   2 = Fair   3 = Acceptable   4 = Good   5 = Excellent

Impromptu Speech

Speaker _____ Topic _____ Date _____

DELIVERY	RATING	COMMENTS
Volume of Voice	1 2 3 4 5	_____
Rate of Speech	1 2 3 4 5	_____
Posture	1 2 3 4 5	_____

CONTENT	RATING	COMMENTS
Attention-Getting Opener	1 2 3 4 5	_____
Organization	1 2 3 4 5	_____
Supporting Ideas	1 2 3 4 5	_____
Summary	1 2 3 4 5	_____
Graceful Conclusion	1 2 3 4 5	_____

ADDITIONAL COMMENTS

_____

_____

_____

_____

RATING KEY

1 = Poor   2 = Fair   3 = Acceptable   4 = Good   5 = Excellent

Idiom/Proverb Speech

Speaker _____ Date _____

Idiom/Proverb _____

DELIVERY	RATING	COMMENTS
Adherence to Time Limit	1 2 3 4 5	_____
Eye Contact	1 2 3 4 5	_____
Volume of Voice	1 2 3 4 5	_____
Rate of Speech	1 2 3 4 5	_____

CONTENT	RATING	COMMENTS
Attention-Getting Opener	1 2 3 4 5	_____
Statement of Idiom or Proverb	1 2 3 4 5	_____
Explanation of Idiom or Proverb	1 2 3 4 5	_____
First Example	1 2 3 4 5	_____
Second Example	1 2 3 4 5	_____
Graceful Conclusion	1 2 3 4 5	_____

ADDITIONAL COMMENTS

_____

_____

RATING KEY

1 = Poor   2 = Fair   3 = Acceptable   4 = Good   5 = Excellent